Workers of All Countries, Unite!

Frederick Engels

The Peasant War in Germany

Progress Publishers • Moscow

TRANSLATED FROM THE GERMAN
EDITED BY VIC SCHNEIERSON

Ф. ЭНГЕЛЬС
КРЕСТЬЯНСКАЯ ВОЙНА В ГЕРМАНИИ

На английском языке

REQUEST TO READERS

Progress Publishers would be glad to have your opinion of this book, its translation and design, and any suggestions you may have for future publications.

Please send your comments to 21, Zubovsky Boulevard, Moscow, U.S.S.R.

First printing 1956
Second revised edition 1965
Third printing 1969
Fourth printing 1974
Fifth printing 1977

Printed in the Union of Soviet Socialist Republics

Э $\frac{10101-139}{014(01)-77}$ без объявл.

CONTENTS

Page

F. ENGELS. THE PEASANT WAR IN GERMANY

Preface	7
I	27
II	40
III	63
IV	78
V	83
VI	114
VII	125

APPENDIX

I. F. Engels. The Mark	135
II. F. Engels. On the History of the Prussian Peasantry	154
III. From the Letters of Karl Marx and Frederick Engels	166
Marx to Engels, *April 16, 1856*	166
Marx to Lassalle, *April 19, 1859*	167
Engels to Lassalle, *May 18, 1859*	169
Engels to Marx, *December 15, 1882*	172
Engels to Marx, *December 16, 1882*	173
Engels to Mehring, *July 14, 1893*	174
Engels to Kautsky, *May 21, 1895*	176
IV. From the Manuscripts of Frederick Engels	178
Decay of Feudalism and Rise of National States	178
Ad "Peasant War"	188
Notes on Germany	190
From the Second Manuscript of "Notes on Germany"	196
Name Index	198

FREDERICK ENGELS

THE PEASANT WAR IN GERMANY

PREFACE[1]

The following work was written in London in the summer of 1850, while the impression of the counter-revolution just then completed was still fresh; it appeared in the fifth and sixth issues of the *Neue Rheinische Zeitung. A Politico-Economic Review*, edited by Karl Marx, Hamburg, 1850. My political friends in Germany desire it to be reprinted, and I accede to their desire, because, to my regret, the work is still timely today.

It makes no claim to providing material derived from independent research. On the contrary, the entire subject-matter on the peasant risings and on Thomas Münzer is taken from Zimmermann.[2] His book, despite gaps here and there, is still the best compilation of the factual material. Moreover, old Zimmermann enjoyed his subject. The same revolutionary instinct, which prompted him here to champion the oppressed classes, made him later one of the best of the extreme Left in Frankfurt.[3] It is true that since then he is said to have aged somewhat.[4]

If, nevertheless, Zimmermann's presentation lacks inner connections; if it does not succeed in showing the politico-religious controversies of the times as a reflection of the contemporary class struggles; if it sees in these class strug-

---

[1] The first part of the present preface was written by Engels in February 1870 to the second German edition of *The Peasant War in Germany*, Leipzig, 1870. On July 1, 1874, Engels wrote a supplementary, second part for the third edition, which appeared in Leipzig in 1875.—*Ed.*

[2] W. Zimmermann, *Allgemeine Geschichte des grossen Bauernkrieges*, T. 1-3, Stuttgart, 1841-43.

[3] The Left wing of the Frankfurt National Assembly, which was in sitting during the German Revolution of 1848-49.—*Ed.*

[4] This sentence was added by Engels to the 1875 edition.—*Ed.*

gles only oppressors and oppressed, evil folk and good folk, and the ultimate victory of the evil ones; if its exposition of the social conditions which determined both the outbreak and the outcome of the struggle is extremely defective, it was the fault of the time in which the book came into existence. On the contrary, for its time, it is written quite realistically and is a laudable exception among the German idealist works on history.

My presentation, while sketching the historic course of the struggle only in its bare outlines, attempted to explain the origin of the Peasant War, the position of the various parties that played a part in it, the political and religious theories by which those parties sought to clarify their position in their own minds, and finally the result of the struggle itself as a necessary upshot of the historically established conditions of the social life of these classes; that is to say, it attempted to demonstrate the political structure of the Germany of that time, the revolts against it and the contemporary political and religious theories not as causes but as results of the stage of development of agriculture, industry, land and waterways, commerce in commodities and money then obtaining in Germany. This, the only materialist conception of history, originates not with myself but with Marx, and can also be found in his works on the French Revolution of 1848-49, in the same *Review*, and in *The Eighteenth Brumaire of Louis Bonaparte*.[1]

The parallel between the German Revolution of 1525 and that of 1848-49 was too obvious to be altogether rejected at that time. Nevertheless, despite the uniformity in the course of events, where various local revolts were crushed one after another by one and the same princely army, despite the often ludicrous similarity in the behaviour of the city burghers in both cases, the difference was clear and distinct.

"Who profited by the Revolution of 1525? The *princes*. Who profited by the Revolution of 1848? The *big* princes, Austria and Prussia. Behind the minor princes of 1525 stood

---

[1] *The Class Struggles in France, 1848 to 1850* and *The Eighteenth Brumaire of Louis Bonaparte*. K. Marx and F. Engels, *Selected Works*, Vol. I, Moscow, 1962.

the petty burghers, who chained the princes to themselves by taxes. Behind the big princes of 1850, behind Austria and Prussia, there stand the modern big bourgeois, rapidly getting them under their yoke by means of the national debt. And behind the big bourgeois stand the proletarians."[1]

I regret to have to say that in this paragraph much too much honour was done the German bourgeoisie. Both in Austria and Prussia it has indeed had the opportunity of "rapidly getting" the monarchy "under its yoke by means of the national debt", but nowhere did it ever make use of this opportunity.

The war of 1866 dropped Austria as a boon into the lap of the bourgeoisie.[2] But it does not know how to rule, it is powerless and incapable of anything. It can do only one thing: savagely attack the workers as soon as they begin to stir. It is still at the helm solely because the *Hungarians* need it.

And in Prussia? True, the national debt has increased by leaps and bounds, the deficit has become a permanent feature, state expenditure grows from year to year, members of the bourgeoisie have a majority in the Chamber and without their consent taxes cannot be increased nor loans floated. But where is their power over the state? Only a few months ago, when there was again a deficit, the bourgeoisie occupied a most favourable position. By holding out only just *a little,* they could have forced far-reaching concessions. What do they do? They regard it as a sufficient concession that the government *allows them* to lay at its feet close on nine millions, not for *one* year, oh no, but for *every* year, and for all time to come.

I do not want to blame the poor National-Liberals[3] in the

---

[1] See the final chapter of *The Peasant War in Germany,* p. 130.

[2] Engels refers to the Austro-Prussian war of 1866, which ended in the rout of Austria in the Battle of Sadowa on July 3, 1866. This defeat made the reactionary Austrian rulers adopt a number of bourgeois reforms (the new constitution of 1867, etc.).—*Ed.*

[3] *National-Liberals*—the party of the German, principally Prussian, bourgeoisie, formed late in 1866 after the split of the bourgeois progressivist party, which opposed Bismarck's Junker government. The policy of the National-Liberals reflected the German liberal bourgeoisie's capitulation to Bismarck after he carried out its programme of unifying Germany from above.—*Ed.*

Chamber more than they deserve. I know they have been left in the lurch by those who stand behind them, by the mass of the bourgeoisie. This mass does not *want* to rule. It still has 1848 in its bones.

Why the German bourgeoisie exhibits this astonishing cowardice will be discussed later.

In other respects the above statement has been fully confirmed. Beginning with 1850, the more and more definite recession into the background of the small states, serving now only as levers for Prussian or Austrian intrigues; the increasingly violent struggles for sole rule waged between Austria and Prussia; finally, the forcible settlement of 1866, after which Austria retains her own provinces, while Prussia subjugates directly or indirectly the whole of the North and the three states of the Southwest are left out in the cold for the time being.[1]

In all this grand performance of state nothing but the following is of importance for the German working class:

First, universal suffrage has given the workers the means of being directly represented in the legislative assembly.

Secondly, Prussia has set a good example by swallowing three other crowns held by the grace of God.[2] Even the National-Liberals do not believe that *after* this operation it still possesses the same immaculate crown, held by the grace of God, which it formerly ascribed to itself.

Thirdly, there is now only *one* serious adversary of the revolution in Germany—the Prussian government.

And fourthly, the German-Austrians will now at last have to make up their minds what they want to be, Germans or Austrians; whom they prefer to belong to—Germany or their extra-German transleithan appendages. It has been

---

[1] After its victory in the Austro-Prussian war Junker Prussia gained the upper hand in Germany, and set to unifying it in an anti-revolutionary manner under her own hegemony. In place of the abolished ephemeral German Union, she created the North-German Union, which consisted of 22 states headed by Prussia. Apart from Austria, three South-German states (Bavaria, Baden, Württemberg, as well as Hesse-Darmstadt, Southwestern Germany) remained out of the Union.—*Ed.*

[2] Allusion is made to the kingdom of Hanover, the electorate of Hesse-Cassel and the grand duchy of Nassau, annexed by Prussia in 1867.—*Ed.*

obvious for a long time that they have to give up one or the other, but this has been continually glossed over by the petty-bourgeois democrats.

As regards the other important controversial points relative to 1866, which since then have been thrashed out *ad nauseam* between the National-Liberals on the one hand, and the People's Party[1] on the other, the history of the next few years should prove that these two standpoints are so bitterly hostile to one another solely because they are the opposite poles of the same narrow-mindedness.

The year 1866 has changed almost nothing in the social pattern of Germany. The few bourgeois reforms—uniform weights and measures, freedom of movement, freedom of occupation, etc., all within limits acceptable to the bureaucracy—do not even come up to *what* the bourgeoisie of other West-European countries has long possessed, and leave the main abuse, the system of bureaucratic tutelage, untouched. For the proletariat all legislation concerning freedom of movement, the right of naturalisation, the abolition of passports, *et cetera,* is anyhow made quite illusory by the common police practices.

What is much more important than the grand performance of 1866 is the growth of German industry and commerce, of railways, telegraphs and ocean shipping since

---

[1] The *Volkspartei,* founded in 1865, consisted of the democratic elements among the petty bourgeoisie and, partly, of the bourgeoisie, chiefly of the South-German states. In contrast to the National-Liberals the Volkspartei opposed Prussian hegemony in Germany and advocated a "Greater Germany" that would include Prussia and Austria. While opposing Prussianism and advancing general democratic slogans, the Volkspartei expressed the particular aspirations of some of the German states. By propagating a federative German state, it actually opposed the unification of Germany as an integral centralised democratic republic.

In 1866 the Saxon People's Party joined the Volkspartei. The Saxon People's Party consisting chiefly of workers became the Left wing of the Volkspartei with which it had nothing essentially in common besides anti-Prussian sentiments and the goal of jointly resolving the issue of the national unification of the country by democratic means. Subsequently, this Left wing gravitated towards socialism. The bulk of the party broke away from the petty-bourgeois democrats and took part in forming the Social-Democratic Workers' Party in August 1869. —*Ed.*

1848. However much this progress lags behind that of England, or even of France, during the same period, it is unprecedented for Germany and has accomplished more in twenty years than previously in a whole century. Only now has Germany been drawn, seriously and irrevocably, into *world commerce*. The capital of the industrialists has multiplied rapidly: the social position of the bourgeoisie has risen accordingly. The surest sign of industrial prosperity —*swindling*—has established itself abundantly and chained counts and dukes to its triumphal chariot. German capital is now constructing Russian and Rumanian railways—may it not come to grief!—whereas only fifteen years ago, German railways went begging to English *entrepreneurs*. How, then, is it possible that the bourgeoisie has not conquered political power as well, that it behaves in so cowardly a manner towards the government?

It is the misfortune of the German bourgeoisie to have arrived too late, as is the favourite German manner. The period of its florescence is occurring at a time when the bourgeoisie of the other West-European countries is already politically in decline. In England, the bourgeoisie could get its real representative, Bright, into the government only by an extension of the franchise, whose consequences are bound to put an end to all bourgeois rule. In France, where the bourgeoisie as such, as a class in its entirety, held power for only two years, 1849 and 1850, under the republic, it was able to continue its social existence only by abdicating its political power to Louis Bonaparte and the army. And on account of the enormously increased interaction of the three most advanced European countries, it is today no longer possible for the bourgeoisie to settle down to comfortable political rule in Germany after this rule has outlived its usefulness in England and France.

It is a peculiarity of the bourgeoisie, in contrast to all former ruling classes, that there is a turning point in its development after which every further expansion of its agencies of power, hence primarily of its capital, only tends to make it more and more unfit for political rule. *"Behind the big bourgeois stand the proletarians."* As the bourgeoisie develops its industry, commerce and means of communication it produces the proletariat. At a certain point—which need not be reached everywhere at the same time or at the same stage of development—it begins to notice that its proletarian double is outgrowing it. From that moment on, it loses the strength required for exclusive political rule; it looks around for allies with whom to share its rule, or to whom to cede the whole of its rule, as circumstances may require.

In Germany this turning point came as early as 1848. To be sure, the German bourgeoisie was less frightened by the German proletariat than by the French. The June 1848 battle in Paris showed the bourgeoisie what it ought to expect; the German proletariat was restless enough to prove to it that the seed that would yield the same crop had already been sown to German soil, too; from that day on the edge was taken off all bourgeois political action. The bourgeoisie looked round for allies, sold itself to them regardless of the price—and even today it has not advanced one step.

These allies are all reactionary by nature. There is the monarchy with its army and its bureaucracy; there is the big feudal nobility; there are the little cabbage-Junkers and there are even the priests. With all of these the bourgeoisie made pacts and bargains, if only to save its dear skin, until at last it had nothing left to barter. And the more the proletariat developed, the more it felt as a class and acted as a class, the more faint-hearted did the bourgeois become. When the astonishingly bad strategy of the Prussians triumphed over the astonishingly worse strategy of the Austrians at Sadowa, it was difficult to say who heaved a deeper sigh of relief—the Prussian bourgeois, who was also defeated at Sadowa, or the Austrian.

Our big bourgeois of 1870 still act exactly as the middle burghers of 1525 acted. As to the petty bourgeois, artisans and shopkeepers, they will always be the same. They hope to climb, to swindle their way into the big bourgeoisie; they are afraid of being thrown down into the proletariat. Hovering between fear and hope, they will during the struggle save their precious skin and join the victor when the struggle is over. Such is their nature.

The social and political activity of the proletariat has kept pace with the upsurgence of industry since 1848. The role that the German workers play today in their trade unions, co-operative societies, political associations and at meetings, elections and in the so-called Reichstag, is by itself sufficient proof of the transformation Germany has imperceptibly undergone in the last twenty years. It redounds to the credit of the German workers that *they alone* have succeeded in sending workers and workers' representatives into parliament—a feat which neither the French nor the English have so far accomplished.

But even the proletariat has not yet outgrown the parallel of 1525. The class exclusively dependent on wages all its life is still far from being the majority of the German people. It is, therefore, also compelled to seek allies. These are to be found only among the petty bourgeoisie, the lumpenproletariat of the cities, the small peasants and the agricultural labourers.

The *petty bourgeois* we have spoken of above. They are extremely unreliable except after a victory has been won, when their shouting in the beer houses knows no bounds. Nevertheless, there are very good elements among them, who join the workers of their own accord.

The *lumpenproletariat,* this scum of depraved elements from all classes, with headquarters in the big cities, is the worst of all the possible allies. This rabble is absolutely venal and absolutely brazen. If the French workers, in every revolution, inscribed on the houses: *Mort aux voleurs!* Death to thieves! and even shot some, they did it not out of reverence for property, but because they rightly considered it necessary above all to get rid of that gang. Every leader of the workers who uses these scoundrels as guards or relies on them for support proves himself by this action alone a traitor to the movement.

The *small peasants*—for the bigger peasants belong to the bourgeoisie—differ in kind.

They are either *feudal peasants* and still have to perform corvée services for their gracious lord. Now that the bourgeoisie has failed in its duty of freeing these people from serfdom, it will not be difficult to convince them that they can expect salvation only from the working class.

Or they are *tenant farmers.* In the latter case the situation is for the most part the same as in Ireland. Rents are pushed so high that in times of average crops the peasant and his family can barely make ends meet; when the crops are bad he is on the verge of starvation, is unable to pay his rent and is consequently entirely at the mercy of the landlord. The bourgeoisie never does anything for these people, unless it is compelled to. From whom then should they expect salvation if not from the workers?

There remain the peasants who cultivate their *own little patches of land*. In most cases they are so burdened with mortgages that they are as dependent on the usurer as the tenant on the landlord. For them also there remains only a meagre wage, which, moreover, since there are good years and bad years, is highly uncertain. These people have least of all to expect anything from the bourgeoisie, because it is precisely the bourgeoisie, the capitalist usurers, who suck the lifeblood out of them. Still, most of these peasants cling to their property, though in reality it does not belong to them but to the usurer. It will have to be brought home to them all the same that they can be freed from the usurer only when a government dependent on the people has transformed all mortgages into debts to the state, and thereby lowered the interest rates. And this can be brought about only by the working class.

Wherever medium-sized and large estates prevail, *farm labourers* form the most numerous class in the countryside. This is the case throughout the North and East of Germany and it is *there* that the industrial workers of the towns find their *most numerous and most natural allies*. In the same way as the capitalist confronts the industrial worker, the landowner or large tenant confronts the farm labourer. The same measures that help the one must also help the other. The industrial workers can free themselves only by transforming the capital of the bourgeois, that is, the raw materials, machines and tools, and the means of subsistence they need to work in production, into the property of society, that is, into their own property, used by them in common. Similarly, the farm labourers can be rescued from their hideous misery only when, primarily, their chief object of labour, the land itself, is withdrawn from the private ownership of the big peasants and the still bigger feudal lords, transformed into public property and cultivated by co-operative associations of agricultural workers on their common account. Here we come to the famous decision of the International Working Men's Congress in Basle[1] that it is in the interest of society to transform landed property into common, national property. This resolution was adopted mainly for countries where there is big landed property, and where, consequently, these big estates are operated by one master and many laboureres. This state of affairs, however, is still largely predominant in Germany, and therefore, next to England, the decision was *most timely precisely for Germany*. The agricultural proletariat, the farm labourers— that is the class from which the bulk of the armies of the princes is recruited. It is the class which, thanks to universal suffrage, sends into parliament the numerous feudal lords and Junkers; but it is also the class nearest to the industrial workers of the towns, which shares their living conditions and is steeped even more in misery than they. To galvanise and draw into the movement this class, impotent because split and scattered, is the immediate and most urgent task of the German labour movement. Its latent power is so well known to the government and nobility that they let the schools fall into decay deliberately in order to keep it ignorant. The day the farm labourers will have learned to understand their own interests, a reactionary, feudal, bureaucratic or bourgeois government will become impossible in Germany.

* * *

The preceding passage was written over four years ago. It is still valid today. What was true after Sadowa and the partition of Germany is being reconfirmed after Sedan and the establishment of the Holy German Empire of the Prussian nation.[2] So little do "world-shaking" grand perform-

---

[1] The Basle Congress of the 1st International took place in September 1869.—*Ed.*

[2] Engels means the proclamation of the German Empire on January 18, 1871, at Versailles, which made Wilhelm I, King of Prussia, the German Emperor following the defeat of Napoleon III at Sedan (September 2, 1870) in the Franco-Prussian war of 1870-71. The founding of the German Empire completed the unification of Germany under the reactionary Prussian Junkerdom and military-bureaucratic caste.—*Ed.*

ances of state in the realm of so-called high politics change the direction of the historical movement!

What these grand performances of state are able to do, however, is to accelerate this movement. And in this respect, the authors of the above-mentioned "world-shaking events" have had involuntary successes, which they themselves surely find most undesirable but which, all the same, for better or for worse, they have to accept.

The war of 1866 shook the old Prussia to its foundations. After 1848 it had a hard time bringing the rebellious industrial element of the Western provinces, bourgeois as well as proletarian, under the old discipline again; still, this had been accomplished, and the interests of the Junkers of the Eastern provinces again became, next to those of the army, the dominant interests in the state. In 1866 almost all Northwest Germany became Prussian. Apart from the irreparable moral injury the Prussian crown suffered by the grace of God owing to its having swallowed three other crowns by the grace of God, the centre of gravity in the monarchy now shifted considerably to the west. The five million Rhinelanders and Westphalians were reinforced, first, by the four million Germans annexed directly, and then by the six million annexed indirectly, through the North-German Union. And in 1870 there were further added the eight million Southwest Germans, so that in the "New Reich", the fourteen and a half million old Prussians (from the six East Elbian provinces, including, besides, two million Poles) were confronted by some twenty-five million who had long outgrown the old Prussian Junker-feudalism. In this way the very victories of the Prussian army shifted the entire basis of the Prussian state structure; the Junker domination became intolerable even for the government. At the same time, however, the extremely rapid industrial development caused the struggle between bourgeois and worker to supersede the struggle between Junker and bourgeois, so that internally also the social foundations of the old state underwent a complete transformation. The basic precondition for the monarchy, which had been slowly rotting since 1840, was the struggle between nobility and bourgeoisie, in which the monarchy held the balance. When the nobility no longer needed protection against the onrush of the bourgeoisie and it became necessary to protect all the propertied classes against the onrush of the working class, the old, absolute monarchy had to go over completely to the form of state expressly devised for this purpose: *the Bonapartist monarchy.* This transition of Prussia to Bonapartism I have already discussed elsewhere *(The Housing Question,* Part 2, pp. 26 et seq.).[1] What I did not have to stress there, but what is very essential here, is that this transition was the *greatest progress* made by Prussia since 1848, so much had Prussia lagged behind in modern development. It was, to be sure, still a semi-feudal state, whereas Bonapartism is, at any rate, a modern form of state which presupposes the abolition of feudalism. Hence, Prussia has had to begin to get rid of its numerous survivals of feudalism, to sacrifice Junkerdom as such. This, natural-

---

[1] Engels refers to the following lines in the second part of *The Housing Question* (published in three editions in Leipzig in 1872-73): "In Prussia—and Prussia is now decisive—there exists side by side with a landowning aristocracy, which is still powerful, a comparatively young and extremely cowardly bourgeoisie, which up to the present has not won either direct political domination, as in France, or more or less indirect domination, as in England. Side by side with these two classes, however, there exists a rapidly increasing proletariat which is intellectually highly developed and which is becoming more and more organised every day. We therefore find here alongside the basic condition of the old absolute monarchy—an equilibrium between the landed aristocracy and the bourgeoisie—the basic condition of modern Bonapartism—an equilibrium between the bourgeoisie and the proletariat. But both in the old absolute monarchy and in the modern Bonapartist monarchy the real governmental authority is held by a special caste of army officers and state officials. In Prussia this caste is replenished partly from its own ranks, partly from the lesser primogenitary aristocracy, more rarely from the higher aristocracy, and least of all from the bourgeoisie. The independence of this caste, which appears to occupy a position outside and, so to speak, above society, gives the state the semblance of independence in relation to society.

The form of state which has developed with the necessary consistency in Prussia (and, following the Prussian example, in the new Reich constitution of Germany) out of these contradictory social conditions is pseudo-constitutionalism, a form which is at once the present-day form of the dissolution of the old absolute monarchy, and the form of existence of the Bonapartist monarchy." (*The Housing Question,* K. Marx and F. Engels, *Selected Works,* Vol. I, Moscow, 1962, p. 605).—*Ed.*

ly, is being done in the mildest possible form and to the favourite tune of: *Immer langsam voran*! Take the notorious District Ordinance. It abolishes the feudal privileges of the individual Junker in relation to his estate only to restore them as privileges of the totality of big landowners in relation to the entire district. The substance remains, being merely translated from the feudal into the bourgeois dialect. The old Prussian Junker is being forcibly transformed into something resembling an English squire, and need not have offered so much resistance because the one is as stupid as the other.

Thus it has been the peculiar fate of Prussia to complete its bourgeois revolution—begun in 1808 to 1813 and advanced to some extent in 1848—in the pleasant form of Bonapartism at the end of this century. If all goes well and the world remains nice and quiet, and all of us live long enough, we may see—perhaps in 1900—that the government of Prussia will actually have abolished all feudal institutions and that Prussia will finally have arrived at the point where France stood in 1792.

The abolition of feudalism, expressed positively, means the establishment of bourgeois conditions. As the privileges of the nobility fall, legislation becomes more and more bourgeois. And here we come to the crux of the relation of the German bourgeoisie to the government. We have seen that the government is *compelled* to introduce these slow and petty reforms. However, in its dealings with the bourgeoisie it portrays each of these small concessions as a *sacrifice* made to the bourgeois, as a concession wrung from the crown with the greatest difficulty, for which the bourgeois ought in return to concede something to the government. And the bourgeois, though the true state of affairs is fairly clear to them, allow themselves to be fooled. This is the origin of the tacit agreement that forms the mute basis of all Reichstag and Prussian Chamber debates in Berlin. On the one hand, the government reforms the laws at a snail's pace in the interest of the bourgeoisie, removes the feudal obstacles to industry as well as those which arose from the multiplicity of small states, establishes uniform coinage, weights and measures, freedom of occupation, etc., puts Germany's labour power at the unrestricted disposal of capital by granting freedom of movement, and favours trade and swindling. On the other hand, the bourgeoisie leaves all actual political power in the hands of the government, votes taxes, loans and soldiers, and helps to frame all new reform laws in a way as to sustain the full force and effect of the old police power over undesirable elements. The bourgeoisie buys gradual social emancipation at the price of the immediate renunciation of political power. Naturally, the chief reason why such an agreement is acceptable to the bourgeoisie is not fear of the government but fear of the proletariat.

However wretched a figure our bourgeoisie may cut in the political field, it cannot be denied that as far as industry and commerce are concerned it is at last doing its duty. The impetuous growth of industry and commerce referred to in the introduction to the second edition has since proceeded with still greater vigour. What has taken place in this respect since 1869 in the Rhine-Westphalian industrial region is quite unprecedented for Germany and reminds one of the upsurge in the English manufacturing districts at the beginning of this century. The same thing holds true for Saxony and Upper Silesia, Berlin, Hanover and the seaports. At last we have world trade, a really big industry, a really modern bourgeoisie. But in return we have also had a real crash, and have likewise got a real, powerful proletariat.

The future historian will attach much less importance in the history of Germany since 1869-74 to the roar of battle at Spichern, Mars-la-Tour[1] and Sedan, and everything connected therewith, than to the unpretentious, quiet but constantly progressing development of the German proletariat. As early as 1870, the German workers were subjected to a severe test: the Bonapartist war provocation and its natu-

---

[1] The battle at Spichern (Lorraine) was one of the first big battles of the Franco-Prussian war of 1870-71. It took place on August 6, 1870, and the Prussian troops inflicted a defeat on the French.
The battle at Mars-la-Tour took place on August 16, 1870. As a result of this battle the Germans succeeded in stopping the retreat of the French Rhine army from Metz and, subsequently, in cutting it off.—*Ed.*

ral effect, the general national enthusiasm in Germany. The German socialist workers did not allow themselves to be confused for a single moment. They did not show any hint of national chauvinism. They kept their heads in the midst of the wildest jubilation over the victory, demanding "an equitable peace with the French republic and no annexations". Not even martial law could silence them. No battle glory, not talk of German "imperial magnificence", produced any effect on them; liberation of the entire European proletariat was still their sole aim. We may say with assurance that in no other country have the workers hitherto been put to so hard a test and acquitted themselves so splendidly.

Martial law during the war was followed by trials for treason, for *lèse majesté,* for insulting officials, and by the ever increasing police chicanery of peacetime. The *Volksstaat* usually had three or four editors in prison at one time and the other papers too. Every party speaker of any distinction had to stand trial at least once a year and was almost always convicted. Deportations, confiscations and the breaking-up of meetings proceeded in rapid succession, thick as hail. All in vain. The place of every man arrested or deported was at once filled by another; for every broken-up meeting two new ones were called, and thus the arbitrary power of the police was worn down in one place after the other by endurance and strict conformity to the law. All this persecution had the opposite effect to that intended. Far from breaking the workers' party or even bending it, it served only to enlist new recruits and consolidated the organisation. In their struggle with the authorities and also individual bourgeois, the workers showed themselves intellectually and morally superior, and proved, particularly in their conflicts with the so-called "providers of work", the employers, that they, the workers, were now the educated class and the capitalists were the ignoramuses. They conduct the fight for the most part with a sense of humour, which is the best proof of how sure they are of their cause and how conscious of their superiority. A struggle thus conducted on historically prepared soil must yield good results. The successes of the January elections stand unique in the history of the modern workers' movement and the astonishment they caused throughout Europe was fully justified.[1]

The German workers have two important advantages over those of the rest of Europe. First, they belong to the most theoretical people of Europe, and have retained the sense of theory which the so-called "educated" classes of Germany have almost completely lost. Without German philosophy, particularly that of Hegel, German scientific socialism—the only scientific socialism that has ever existed—would never have come into being. Without the workers' sense of theory this scientific socialism would never have entered their flesh and blood as much as is the case. What an incalculable advantage this is may be seen, on the one hand, from the indifference to theory which is one of the main reasons why the English working-class movement crawls along so slowly in spite of the splendid organisation of the individual trades, and on the other hand, from the mischief and confusion wrought by Proudhonism in its original form among the French and Belgians, and in the form further caricatured by Bakunin among the Spaniards and Italians.

The second advantage is that, chronologically speaking, the Germans were about the last to come into the workers' movement. Just as German theoretical socialism will never forget that it rests on the shoulders of Saint-Simon, Fourier and Owen—three men who, in spite of all their fantastic notions and all their utopianism, stand among the most eminent thinkers of all time and whose genius anticipated innumerable things the correctness of which is now being scientifically proved by us—so the practical workers' movement in Germany ought never to forget that it developed on the shoulders of the English and French movements, that it was able simply to utilise their dearly paid experience and could now avoid their mistakes, which were then mostly unavoidable. Where would we be now without the precedent of the English trade unions and French work-

---

[1] Nine Social-Democrats were elected in the Reichstag elections on January 10, 1874, polling more than 350,000 or 6 per cent of all votes. Among the elected were A. Bebel and W. Liebknecht, who were then serving prison terms.—*Ed.*

ers' political struggles, and especially without the gigantic impulse of the Paris Commune?

It must be said to the credit of the German workers that they have exploited the advantages of their situation with rare understanding. For the first time since a workers' movement has existed, the struggle is being waged pursuant to its three sides—the theoretical, the political and the economico-practical (resistance to the capitalists)—in harmony and in its interconnections, and in a systematic way. It is precisely in this, as it were concentric, attack that the strength and invincibility of the German movement lies.

Due to this advantageous situation, on the one hand, and to the insular peculiarities of the English and the forcible suppression of the French movement, on the other, the German workers stand for the moment in the vanguard of the proletarian struggle. How long events will allow them to occupy this place of honour, cannot be foretold. But let us hope that as long as they occupy it they will fill it fittingly. This demands redoubled efforts in every field of struggle and agitation. In particular, it will be the duty of the leaders to gain an ever clearer insight into all theoretical questions, to free themselves more and more from the influence of traditional phrases inherited from the old world outlook, and constantly to keep in mind that socialism, since it has become a science, demands that it be pursued as a science, that is, that it be studied. The task will be to spread with increased zeal among the masses of workers the ever more lucid understanding thus acquired and to knit together ever more strongly the organisation both of the party and of the trade unions. Even if the votes cast for the Socialists in January have formed quite a decent army, they are still far from constituting the majority of the working class; encouraging as are the successes of propaganda among the rural population, infinitely more remains to be done in this field. Hence, we must make it a point not to slacken the struggle, and to wrest from the enemy one town, one constituency after the other; the main point, however, is to safeguard the true international spirit, which allows no patriotic chauvinism to arise and which readily welcomes every new advance of the proletarian movement, no matter from which nation it comes. If the German workers progress in this way, they will not be marching exactly at the head of the movement—it is not at all in the interest of this movement that the workers of any particular country should march at its head—but will occupy an honourable place in the battle line; they will stand armed for battle when either unexpectedly grave trials or momentous events demand of them added courage, added determination and energy.

London, July 1, 1874 *Frederick Engels*

Revolutionary peasant with banner

The German people also have their revolutionary tradition. There was a time when Germany produced characters that could match the best men in the revolutions of other countries, when the German people displayed an endurance and vigour which, in a centralised nation, would have yielded the most magnificent results and when the German peasants and plebeians were full of ideas and plans that often make their descendants shudder.

It is time once more, as a counterweight to the present slackening evident almost everywhere after two years of struggle, to present to the German people the clumsy yet powerful and tenacious figures of the great Peasant War. Three centuries have passed and many a thing has changed; still the Peasant War is not so far removed from our present struggle, and the opponents who have to be fought remain essentially the same. The classes and fractions of classes which everywhere betrayed 1848 and 1849, were in evidence in the role of traitors as early as 1525, though on a lower level of development. It is by no means a credit to the modern insurrection that the robust vandalism of the Peasant War came into its own only here and there in the movement of the last few years—at Odenwald, the Black Forest, and in Silesia.

I

Let us first briefly review the situation in Germany at the beginning of the sixteenth century.

German industry had made considerable progress in the fourteenth and fifteenth centuries. The feudal local countryside industry was superseded by the guild system of industry in the towns, which produced for wider circles, and even for remoter markets. The weaving of coarse woollen fabrics and linens had become a standing and widespread branch of industry, and even finer woollen and linen fabrics and silks were being manufactured in Augsburg. Along with the art of weaving there had developed particularly those branches of industry which, verging on the fine arts, were nurtured by the ecclesiastic and secular luxury of the late medieval epoch: those of the gold- and silver-smith, the sculptor and engraver, etcher and wood-carver, armourer, engraver of medals, wood-turner, etc. A series of more or less important discoveries, the most prominent of which were the invention of gunpowder* and printing, had contributed substantially to the development of the crafts. Commerce kept pace with industry. Through its century-long monopoly of sea navigation, the Hanseatic League[1] assured the elevation of all Northern Germany from medieval barbarism. Even though the Hanseatic League had begun to succumb to the competition of the English and Dutch after the end of the fifteenth century, the great trade route from India to the north still lay through Germany, Vasco da Gama's discoveries notwithstanding, while Augsburg remained an important market for Italian silks, Indian spices, and all Levantine products. The towns of Upper Germany, particularly Augsburg and Nuremberg, were centres of opulence and luxury, quite remarkable for that time. The production of raw materials had also markedly increased. The German miners of the fifteenth century were the most skilful in the world and agriculture had also overcome its early medieval crudity thanks to the flowering of the towns. Not only had large stretches of land been put under cultivation, but dye crops and other imported plants were introduced, whose careful cultivation exerted a generally favourable influence on farming.

---

* As has now been unquestionably determined, gunpowder came to the Arabs through India from China, and they brought it through Spain to Europe along with firearms. *Note by Engels* in the 1875 edition.

[1] *Hanseatic League*—a federation of medieval German towns along the North Sea and Baltic Sea coasts, and their adjoining rivers; it took final shape in the latter half of the 14th century. Hamburg, Lübeck and Bremen played a leading part in the federation.—*Ed.*

Still, the progress of Germany's national production had not kept pace with the progress in other countries. Agriculture lagged far behind that of England and the Netherlands. Industry lagged far behind the Italian, Flemish, and English, and the English, and particularly the Dutch, were already ousting the Germans from the sea trade. The population was still very sparse. Civilisation in Germany existed only in spots, concentrated round the several centres of industry and commerce; but even the interests of these centres diverged, with hardly any point of contact. The trade relations and export markets of the South differed totally from those of the North; the East and the West stood outside all traffic. No single city had grown into an industrial and commercial point of gravity for the whole country, such, for instance, as London had already become for England. All internal communications were almost exclusively confined to coastwise and river navigation and to the few large trade routes from Augsburg and Nuremberg via Cologne to the Netherlands, and via Erfurt to the North. Away from the rivers and trade routes there was a number of smaller towns which lay beyond the major traffic and continued to vegetate undisturbed in the conditions of the late Middle Ages, needing only few foreign goods and yielding few products for export. Of the rural population only the nobility came into contact with wider circles and with new requirements; the peasant masses never overstepped the narrow local relations and the resulting narrow local outlook.

While in England and France the rise of commerce and industry had the effect of fusing the interests of the entire country, and thereby brought about political centralisation, Germany only succeeded in grouping interests by provinces, around purely local centres, which led to political division, a division that was soon made all the more conclusive by Germany's exclusion from world commerce. As the *purely feudal* Empire was falling apart, the bonds of imperial unity broke, the major vassals became almost independent sovereigns, and the cities of the Empire, on the one hand, and the knights of the Empire, on the other, entered into alliances either against each other, or against the princes or the Emperor. Uncertain of its own position, the imperial government vacillated between the various elements comprising the Empire, and thereby lost more and more authority; in spite of all its intrigues and violence, the attempt at centralisation in the manner of Louis XI only just held together the Austrian hereditary lands.[1] The *princes*, representing local and provincial centralisation amidst disunion, at whose side the Emperor gradually became little more than a prince himself, could not help emerging the final winners in this confusion of countless and conflicting clashes.

Under the circumstances, the position of the classes that survived from the Middle Ages changed considerably. New classes took shape beside the old.

The *princes* came from the big aristocracy. They were already almost independent of the Emperor and possessed most of the sovereign rights. They made war and peace all on their own, maintained standing armies, convened Diets, and levied taxes. They brought a large part of the lesser nobility and most of the towns under their sway, and resorted continuously to all possible means of incorporating in their dominion all the remaining imperial towns and baronial estates. They assumed the role of centralisers in respect to such towns and estates, while acting as a decentralising factor with regard to the imperial power. Internally, their reign was already highly autocratic. They convened the Estates only when they could not do without them. They imposed taxes and borrowed money whenever they saw fit; the right of the Estates to ratify taxes was seldom recognised and still more seldom practised. And even then the prince usually had the majority by virtue of the knights and higher clergy, the two Estates that paid no taxes and shared in their benefits. The princes' need for money grew with their taste for luxuries, the extension of their courts, the standing armies, and the mounting costs of administration. The taxes became ever more oppressive. The towns were mostly protected from them by privileges, and the full

---

[1] Those were lands that belonged directly to the Austrian House of Hapsburg. In the 16th century the Austrian Hapsburgs ruled Upper and Lower Austria, Tirol, a number of lands along the Upper Rhine, and such Slav lands as the dukedoms of Styria, Carinthia, and Carniola. Beginning with 1526 their rule spread to the kingdom of Czechia and a part of Hungary.—*Ed.*

impact of the tax burden fell upon their peasant subjects, those of the princes, as well as on the serfs, bondsmen and copyholders[1] of their vassal knights. Whenever direct taxes proved insufficient, indirect taxes were introduced. The most intricate devices of finance were called into play to fill the gaping holes in the treasury. When nothing else availed, when there was nothing to pawn and no free imperial city was willing to grant credit any longer, the princes resorted to currency operations of the basest kind, coined depreciated money, and set high or low compulsory exchange rates at the convenience of their treasuries. Furthermore, trade in urban and other privileges, later forcibly withdrawn only to be re-sold at a higher price, and the use of every attempt at opposition as an excuse for all kinds of extortion and robbery, etc., etc., were common and lucrative sources of income for the princes of that day. Justice was also a standing and not unimportant merchandise. In brief, the subjects of that time, who, in addition, had to satisfy the private avarice of the princely bailiffs and officials, had a full taste of all the blessings of the "paternal" system of government.

The middle nobility of the medieval feudal hierarchy had almost entirely disappeared; it had either risen to acquire the independence of petty princes, or dropped into the ranks of the lesser nobility. The *lesser nobility*, or *knighthood*, was fast moving towards extinction. Much of it was already impoverished and lived in the service of the princes, holding military or civil offices; another part of it was in the vassalage and under the sway of the princes; and a small part was directly subject to the Emperor. The development of military science, the growing importance of the infantry, and the improvement of firearms dwarfed its military merits as heavy cavalry, and also put an end to the invincibility of its castles. Like the Nuremberg artisans, the knights were made superfluous by the progress of industry. The need that the knights had for money added considerably to their ruin. The luxury of their castles, rivalry in the magnificence

---

[1] Dependent peasants, enjoying personal freedom but obliged to pay quitrent for their copyholds and having other obligations to their feudal lord.—*Ed.*

of tournaments and feasts, the price of armaments and horses—all increased with social progress, while the sources of income of the knights and barons increased but little, if at all. As time went on, feuds with their attendant plunder and extortion, highway robbery and similar noble occupations, became too dangerous. The payments and services of their subjects yielded the knights little more than before. In order to satisfy their mounting requirements, the gracious knights had to resort to the same means as the princes. The peasantry was plundered by the nobility with increasing dexterity every year. The serfs were sucked dry, and the bondsmen were burdened with ever new duties on a great variety of pretexts and on all possible occasions. Compulsory labour, dues, ground rents, land sale taxes, death taxes, protection moneys,[1] etc., were raised at will, in spite of old agreements. Justice was denied, or sold for money, and wherever the knight failed to obtain the peasant's money in any other way, he threw him into the tower without further ado and forced him to pay a ransom.

The relations between the lesser nobility and the other Estates were also far from friendly. The knights bound by vassalage to the princes strove to become vassals of the Empire, the imperial knights strove to retain their independence; this led to incessant conflicts with the princes. The knight regarded the arrogant clergy of the day as an entirely superfluous Estate, and envied them their large possessions and the wealth held secure by their celibacy and the church statutes. He was continually at loggerheads with the towns, he was always in debt to them, he made his living by plundering their territory, robbing their merchants, and by holding for ransom prisoners captured in the feuds. The struggle of the knights against all these Estates became the more vehement, the more the money question became a question of life to them as well.

---

[1] *Death taxes* (Sterbefall, Todfall)—taxes levied upon the inheritance on the strength of the feudal seigniorial right on the land and property of the deceased peasant (in France, "the right of the dead hand"). In Germany the feudal lords usually took from the heirs the best head of cattle. *Protection moneys* (Schutzgelder)—a tax levied by feudal lords in payment for the "judicial protection" and "patronage" which the seignior claimed to extend to his subjects.—*Ed.*

The *clergy,* that bearer of the medieval feudal ideology, felt the influence of historic change no less acutely. Printing and the claims of extended commerce robbed it of its monopoly not only on reading and writing, but also on higher education. The division of labour also made inroads into the realm of intellectual work. The newly rising juridical Estate drove the clergy from a number of extremely influential positions. The clergy was also on its way to becoming largely superfluous, and demonstrated it with its ever growing laziness and ignorance. But the more superfluous it became, the more it grew in number, due to the enormous riches that it still continuously augmented by all possible means.

There were two distinct classes among the clergy. The clerical feudal hierarchy formed the *aristocratic* class: the bishops and archbishops, abbots, priors, and other prelates. These high church dignitaries were either imperial princes themselves, or reigned as feudal lords under the sovereignty of other princes over extensive lands with numerous serfs and bondsmen. They not only exploited their dependents as ruthlessly as the knights and princes, but went at it with even less shame. Alongside brute force they applied all the subterfuges of religion, alongside the fear of the rack they applied the fear of ex-communication and the refusal of absolution; they made use of all the intrigues of the confessional to wring the last penny from their subjects, or to multiply the portion of the church. Forgery of documents was their common and favourite means of swindling. But although they received tithes from their subjects in addition to the usual feudal payments and quitrents, they were in constant need of money. They resorted to the fabrication of miracle-working sacred images and relics, set up sanctifying prayer-houses, and traded in indulgences, all in order to squeeze more money out of the people, and for quite some time with no little success.

It was these prelates and their numerous gendarmerie of monks, which grew constantly with the spread of political and religious witch-hunts, on whom the priest-hatred not only of the people, but also of the nobility, was concentrated. They were in the way of the princes, being directly subject to the Emperor. The life of luxurious pleasure led by the corpulent bishops and abbots, and their army of monks roused the envy of the nobility and the indignation of the people, who had to bear its cost; and the greater the indignation, the greater the contrast became between their practice and their preaching.

The *plebeian* part of the clergy consisted of rural and urban preachers. These stood outside the feudal church hierarchy and had no part in its riches. Their work was less controlled, and, important as it was for the church, it was for the moment far less indispensable than the police services of the barracked monks. They were, therefore, the worse paid by far, compared with the monks, and their prebends were mostly very scanty. Of burgher or plebeian origin, they stood close enough to the life of the masses to retain their burgher and plebeian sympathies in spite of their clerical status. While monks were an exception in the movements of their time, the plebeian clergy was the rule. They provided the movement with theorists and ideologists, and many of them, representatives of the plebeians and peasants, died on the scaffold. The popular hatred for the clergy turned against them only in isolated cases.

What the Emperor was to the princes and nobility, the *Pope* was to the higher and lower clergy. Just as the Emperor received the "general pfennig",[1] or the imperial taxes, so the Pope received the universal church taxes, out of which he defrayed the cost of the luxury at the Roman court. Thanks to the power and number of the clergy, these church taxes were in no country collected so conscientiously and rigorously as in Germany. And particularly the annates, collected when bishoprics were conferred.[2] The mounting requirements led to the invention of new means of raising revenues, such as the trade in relics and indulgences, jubilee collections, etc. Large sums of money flowed yearly

---

[1] *"General pfennig"* (gemeiner Pfennig)—a tax introduced by Emperor Maximilian I, which was a combination of poll-tax and tax on property. The main burden of this tax fell on the peasantry.—*Ed.*

[2] *Annates* were the first fruits of a benefice paid to the Pope by persons whom he appointed to church offices. They were in most cases equal to a year's revenue of the benefice, whose holders reimbursed themselves a hundredfold in taxes and extortions from the population. —*Ed.*

from Germany to Rome in this way, and the consequent increased oppression not only fanned the hatred for the clergy, but also roused the national sentiments, particularly of the nobility, that most nationalistic Estate of the day.

In the cities, three distinct groups developed from the original citizenry of the medieval *towns* with the growth of commerce and the handicrafts.

The town community was headed by the *patriciate,* the so-called "*honourables*". They were the richest families. They alone sat in the town council, and held all town offices. Hence, they not only administered all the town revenues, but also consumed them. Strong by virtue of their wealth and time-honoured aristocratic status, which was recognised by Emperor and Empire, they exploited the town community and the peasants belonging to the town in every possible way. They practised usury in grain and money, seized monopolies of all kinds, gradually deprived the community of all rights to commonable town forests and meadows, and utilised them exclusively for their own private benefit, exacted arbitrary road-, bridge- and gate-tolls, and other imposts, and trafficked in trade, guild, and burgher privileges, and in justice. They treated the peasants of the town precincts with no greater consideration than the nobility and clergy. What is more, town bailiffs and officials in the village, patricians all, added a certain bureaucratic punctiliousness to aristocratic rigidity and avarice in collecting imposts. The town revenues thus collected were administered in a most arbitrary fashion; the accounts in the town books, a mere formality, were neglected and confused to the extreme; embezzlement and deficit were the order of the day. How easy it was at that time for a comparatively small, privileged caste bound by family ties and common interests, to enrich itself enormously out of the town revenues, will be seen from the numerous embezzlements and swindles which 1848 brought to light in so many town administrations.

The patricians took pains everywhere to let the rights of the town community fall into disuse, particularly in matters of finance. Only later, when their machinations overstepped all bounds, the communities came into motion again to at least control the town administration. In most towns they actually regained their rights, but due to the eternal squabbles between the guilds, the tenacity of the patricians, and the protection the latter enjoyed from the Empire and the governments of the allied towns, the patrician council members soon regained their former undivided dominance in the councils, be it by cunning, or force. At the beginning of the sixteenth century the communities in all the towns were again in the opposition.

The town opposition to the patricians broke up into two factions which took quite distinct stands in the Peasant War.

The *burgher opposition,* forerunners of the present-day liberals, included the richer and middle burghers, and, depending on local conditions, a more or less appreciable section of the petty burghers. Their demands did not overstep purely constitutional bounds. They wanted control over the town administration and a hand in legislative power, to be exercised either by a general meeting of the community itself, or by its representatives (big council, community committee); further, restriction of the patrician nepotism and oligarchy of a few families which was coming to the fore ever more openly within the patriciate itself. At best, they demanded several council seats for burghers from their own midst. This party, joined here and there by the dissatisfied and impoverished part of the patriciate, had a large majority in all the ordinary community assemblies and in the guilds. The adherents of the Council and the more radical part of the opposition together formed only a minority among the real *burghers*.

We shall see how this "moderate", "law-abiding", "well-to-do" and "intelligent" opposition played exactly the same role, with exactly the same effect, in the movement of the sixteenth century, as its successor, the Constitutional Party, played in the movement of 1848 and 1849.[1]

---

[1] Engels alludes to the German bourgeois liberals who were in the majority in the Frankfurt National Assembly and in some German states during the Revolution of 1848-49. In the first months of the revolution liberals headed "constitutional governments" in a number of states (Prussia, for example), but were later replaced by representatives of the bureaucracy and nobility. The liberals sought to preserve the monarchy as a stronghold against the further spread and develop-

Beyond that, the burgher opposition declaimed zealously against the clergy, whose idle luxury and loose morals roused its bitter scorn. It called for measures against the scandalous life of those worthy men. It demanded the abolition of the clergy's special jurisdiction and freedom from taxes, and particularly, a reduction in the number of monks.

The *plebeian opposition* consisted of ruined burghers and the mass of townsmen deprived of civic rights—journeymen, day labourers, and the numerous precursors of the lumpenproletariat, who may be found even in the lowest stages of urban development. The lumpenproletariat is, generally speaking, a phenomenon evident in a more or less developed form in all the phases of society to date. The number of people without a definite occupation and a stable domicile increased greatly at that time, due to the decay of feudalism in a society in which every occupation, every sphere of life, was still fenced in by countless privileges. The vagabonds in all the developed countries were never so numerous as in the first half of the sixteenth century. In war-time some of these tramps joined the armies, others begged their way across the countryside, and still others eked out a meagre living in the towns as day labourers or from whatever else was not under guild jurisdiction. All three groups played a part in the Peasant War—the first in the armies of princes which overpowered the peasants, the second in the peasant conspiracies and peasant troops, where its demoralising influence was felt at all times, and the third in the clashes of the urban parties. It will be recalled, however, that a great many, namely those living in the towns, still had a substantial share of sound peasant nature and had not as yet been possessed by the venality and depravity of the present "civilised" lumpenproletariat.

Plainly, the plebeian opposition in the towns of that day was mixed. It brought together the depraved elements of the old feudal and guild society with the undeveloped, budding proletarian elements of the bourgeoning modern bour-

---

ment of the revolution. The conciliatory tactics of the bourgeois constitutionalists, and their traitorous deals with reactionary parties, were one of the chief reasons for the defeat of the German revolution.—*Ed.*

geois society. There were impoverished guild burghers, on the one hand, who still clung to the existing burgher system by virtue of their privileges, and dispossessed peasants and discharged vassals as yet unable to become proletarians, on the other. Between these two groups were the journeymen, who stood outside official society for the time being and whose living conditions were very much like those of the proletariat by virtue of the contemporary state of industry and the guild privileges; but due to these privileges, they were, at the same time, almost all prospective burgher artisans. The party affiliations of this conglomeration were therefore highly uncertain, and varied from locality to locality. Before the Peasant War the plebeian opposition took part in the political struggles not as a party, but as a noisy marauding tagtail of the burgher opposition, a mob that could be bought and sold for a few barrels of wine. The peasant revolts turned it into a party, and even then it remained almost everywhere dependent on the peasants in its demands and actions—a striking proof of how much the town of that time still depended on the countryside. So far as their independent actions went, the plebeians demanded an extension of the monopolies of urban handicrafts to the countryside, and had no wish to see a curtailment of town revenues come about through the abolition of feudal burdens within the town precincts, etc.; in brief, they were reactionary so far as independent actions went, and delivered themselves up to their own petty bourgeois elements—a typical prelude to the comedy staged in the last three years by the modern petty bourgeoisie under the trade mark of democracy.

Only in Thuringia under the direct influence of Münzer, and in a few other localities under that of his pupils, was the plebeian faction of the towns carried away by the general storm to such an extent that the embryonic proletarian element in it gained the upper hand for a time over all the other factions of the movement. This episode, grouped about the magnificent figure of *Thomas Münzer*, was the culmination point of the Peasant War, and also the briefest. It stands to reason that the plebeian factions were the quickest to collapse, that they bore a distinctly fantastic stamp, and that their demands were necessarily expressed with extreme uncertainty; in the existing conditions they found the least firm ground to stand on.

At the bottom of all these classes, save the last one, was the exploited bulk of the nation, the *peasants*. It was the peasant who supported the other strata of society: princes, officials, nobles, clergymen, patricians and burghers. No matter whose subject the peasant was—a prince's, an imperial baron's, a bishop's, a monastery's or a town's—he was treated by all as a thing, a beast of burden, and worse. If he was a serf, he was entirely at the mercy of his master. If he was a bondsman, the legal levies stipulated in the agreement were sufficient to crush him; and yet they were daily increased. He had to work on his lord's estate most of his time; out of what he earned in his few free hours he had to pay tithes, dues, ground rents, road (war) imposts, and local and imperial taxes. He could neither marry, nor die, without paying the lord. Besides his statute labour he had to gather litter, pick strawberries and bilberries, collect snail-shells, drive the game in the hunt, and chop wood, ets., for his lord. The right to fish and hunt belonged to the master; the peasant had to stand quietly by and watch his crop destroyed by wild game. The common pastures and woods of the peasants were almost everywhere forcibly appropriated by the lord. The lord reigned as he pleased over the peasant's own person, over his wife and daughters, just as he reigned over his property. He had the right of the first night. He threw the peasant into the tower whenever he saw fit, and the rack awaited the peasant there just as surely as the investigating attorney awaits the arrested in our day. He killed the peasant, or had him beheaded, whenever he pleased. There was no instructive chapter of the Carolina regarding "ear clipping", "nose cutting", "eye gouging", "chopping of fingers and hands", "beheading", "breaking on the wheel", "burning", "hot irons", "quartering", etc., that the gracious lord and patron would not apply at will. Who would defend the peasant? It was barons, clergymen, patricians, or jurists, who sat in the courts, and they knew perfectly well what they were being paid for. All the official Estates of the Empire, after all, lived by squeezing dry the peasants.

Although gnashing their teeth under the terrible burden,

the peasants were difficult to rouse to revolt. They were scattered over large areas, and this made every agreement between them extremely difficult; the old habit of submission inherited by generation from generation, lack of practice in the use of arms in many regions, and the varying degree of exploitation depending on the personality of the lord, all combined to keep the peasant quiet. For this reason we find so many local peasant insurrections in the Middle Ages, but, prior to the Peasant War, not a single general national peasant revolt, at least in Germany. Moreover, the peasants alone were unable to start a revolution as long as they were confronted by the united and organised power of the princes, the nobility and the towns. Their only chance of victory lay in an alliance with other Estates. But how could they join hands with other Estates if they were exploited by all?

In the early sixteenth century the various Estates of the Empire—princes, nobles, prelates, patricians, burghers, plebeians and peasants—formed an extremely confusing mass with their varied and highly conflicting requirements. The Estates stood in each other's way, and each was continually in overt, or covert, conflict with all the others. The division of the nation into two distinct camps, as seen in France at the outbreak of the first Revolution and as witnessed today on a higher stage of development in the most advanced countries, was a rank impossibility under the circumstances. Anything like it could only come about if the lowest stratum of the nation, the one exploited by all the other Estates, the peasants and plebeians, would rise. The entanglement which involved interests, views and aspirations of that time will be easily understood from the confusion reigning in the last two years in the present, far less complicated structure of the German nation, consisting of the feudal nobility, the bourgeoisie, the petty bourgeoisie, the peasants and the proletariat.

II

The grouping of the then numerous and different Estates into bigger entities was made virtually impossible by decentralisation, local and provincial independence, the industrial and commercial isolation of the provinces from each other, and poor communications. It proceeded only with the general spread of revolutionary, politico-religious ideas during the Reformation. The various Estates that either embraced or opposed those ideas, concentrated the nation, painfully and only approximately, into three large camps— the reactionary or Catholic camp, the Lutheran bourgeois reformist camp, and the revolutionary camp. Should we discover little logic in this great division of the nation, and partly find the same elements in the first two camps, this is explained by the dissolution of most of the official Estates come down from the Middle Ages, and by the decentralisation which, for the moment, imparted to these Estates in different localities opposing tendencies. In recent years we have so often encountered similar facts in Germany that this apparent jumble of Estates and classes in the much more complicated environment of the sixteenth century can scarcely surprise us.

In spite of the latest experiences, the German ideology still sees nothing except violent theological bickering in the struggles that ended the Middle Ages. Should the people of that time, say our home-bred historians and sages, have only come to an understanding concerning divine matters, there would have been no reason whatever for quarrelling over earthly affairs. These ideologists are gullible enough to accept unquestioningly all the illusions that an epoch makes about itself, or that ideologists of some epoch make about that epoch. People of that kind see nothing in, say, the Revolution of 1789 but a somewhat heated debate over the advantages a constitutional monarchy has over absolutism, in the July Revolution a practical controversy over the untenability of justice "by the grace of God", and in the February Revolution an attempt at solving the problem: republic or monarchy?, etc. They have hardly any idea to this day of the *class struggles* fought out in these upheavals, of which the political slogan on the banner is every time a bare expression, although notice of them is audible enough not only from abroad but also in the roar and rumble of many thousands of home proletarians.

Even the so-called religious wars of the sixteenth century involved positive material class interests; those wars were class wars, too, just as the later internal collisions in England and France. Although the class struggles of that day were clothed in religious shibboleths, and though the interests, requirements, and demands of the various classes were concealed behind a religious screen, this changed nothing and is easily explained by the conditions of the time.

The Middle Ages had developed altogether from the raw. They wiped the old civilisation, the old philosophy, politics and jurisprudence off the state, to begin anew in everything. The only thing they kept from the shattered old world was Christianity and a number of half-ruined towns divested of all civilisation. As a consequence, the clergy obtained a monopoly on intellectual education, just as in every primitive stage of development, and education itself became essentially theological. In the hands of the clergy politics and jurisprudence, much like all other sciences, remained mere branches of theology, and were treated in accordance with the principles prevailing in the latter. Church dogmas were also political axioms, and Bible quotations had the validity of law in any court. Even as a special Estate of jurists was taking shape, jurisprudence long remained under the patronage of theology. This domination of theology over the entire realm of intellectual activity was at the same time an inevitable consequence of the fact that the church was the all-embracing synthesis and the most general sanction of the existing feudal domination.

It is clear that under the circumstances all the generally voiced attacks against feudalism, above all the attacks against the church, and all revolutionary social and political doctrines had mostly and simultaneously to be theological heresies. The existing social relations had to be stripped of their halo of sanctity before they could be attacked.

The revolutionary opposition to feudalism was alive all down the Middle Ages. It took the shape of mysticism, open heresy, or armed insurrection, all depending on the conditions of the time. As for mysticism, it is well known how much sixteenth-century reformers depended on it. Münzer himself was largely indebted to it. The heresies gave expression partly to the reaction of the patriarchal Alpine shepherds against the feudalism advancing upon them

(Waldenses[1]), partly to the opposition of the towns that had outgrown feudalism (the Albigenses,[2] Arnold of Brescia, etc.), and partly to direct peasant insurrections (John Ball and, among others, the Hungarian teacher[3] in Picardy). We can here leave aside the patriarchal heresy of the Waldenses and the Swiss insurrection, which was in form and content a reactionary, purely local attempt at stemming the tide of history. In the other two forms of medieval heresy we find the twelfth-century precursors of the great antithesis between the burgher and peasant-plebeian oppositions, which caused the defeat of the Peasant War. This antithesis is evident all down the later Middle Ages.

The town heresies—and those are the actual official heresies of the Middle Ages—were turned primarily against the clergy, whose wealth and political importance they attacked. Just as the present-day bourgeoisie demands a *"gouvernement à bon marché"* (cheap government), the medieval burghers chiefly demanded an *"église à bon marché"* (cheap church). Reactionary in form, like any heresy that sees only degeneration in the further development of church and dogma, the burgher heresy demanded the revival of the simple early Christian Church constitution and abolition of exclusive priesthood. This cheap arrangement would eliminate monks, prelates, and the

---

[1] *Waldenses*—a religious sect which originated among the urban lower classes of Southern France in the late 12th century. Its founder is said to have been Peter Wald, a Lyons merchant. The Waldenses advocated abolition of property, condemned the wealth of the Catholic Church, and called for a return to the customs of early Christianity. The heresies of the Waldenses were widespread among the rural population of the mountain regions of Southwestern Switzerland and Savoy, where they tended to uphold the survivals of the primitive communal system and patriarchal relations.—*Ed.*

[2] *Albigenses*—a religious sect widespread in the towns of Southern France and Northern Italy in the 12th and 13th centuries. Its main seat was in the town of Albi in the South of France. The Albigenses, who opposed the sumptuous Catholic rites and the church hierarchy, clothed the protest of the tradesmen and artisans against feudalism in religious terms. They were joined by a section of the Southern French nobility, which sought to secularise church lands. Pope Innocent III organised a crusade against the Albigenses in 1209. The movement was crushed after 20 years of war and brutal persecutions.—*Ed.*

[3] One of the leaders of the peasant revolt in France in 1251 ("Shepherds'" revolt).—*Ed.*

Roman court; in short, all the expensive element of the Church. The towns, which were republics by their own rights, albeit under the protection of monarchs, first enunciated in general terms through their attacks upon the Papacy that a republic was the normal form of bourgeois rule. Their hostility to some of the dogmas and church laws is explained partly by the foregoing, and partly by their living conditions. Their bitter opposition to celibacy, for instance, has never been better explained than by Boccaccio. Arnold of Brescia in Italy and Germany, the Albigenses in Southern France, John Wycliffe in England, Hus and the Calixtines[1] in Bohemia, were the principal exponents of this trend. The towns were then already a recognised Estate sufficiently capable of fighting lay feudalism and its privileges either by force of arms or in the Estate assemblies. This explains quite simply why the opposition to feudalism appeared only as opposition to *religious* feudalism.

We also find in Southern France and in England and Bohemia that most of the lesser nobility joined the towns in their struggle against the clergy and in their heresies—which is explained by the dependence of the lesser nobility on the towns, and by their common interests as opposed to the princes and prelates. We shall encounter the same thing in the Peasant War.

The heresy that lent direct expression to peasant and plebeian demands and was almost invariably associated with an insurrection was of a totally different nature. Though it had all the demands of burgher heresy with

---

[1] *Calixtines* and *Taborites*—two trends in the Hussite national liberation and reformation movement in Bohemia (first half of the 15th century) against the German nobility, the German Empire and the Catholic Church. The Calixtines (who maintained that the laity should receive the cup as well as the bread in the Eucharist), supported by the Czech nobility and burghers, sought no more than a moderate church reform and the secularisation of church estates. The Taborites (so called from their camp, now the town of Tabor, in Bohemia) were the revolutionary democratic wing of the Hussites and in their demands reflected the desire of the peasantry and the urban lower classes to end all feudal oppression. The feudal lords took advantage of the betrayal of the Taborites by the Calixtines to suppress the Hussite movement.—*Ed*.

regard to the clergy, the Papacy and the revival of the early Christian Church constitution, it went infinitely further. It demanded the restoration of early Christian equality among members of the community and recognition of this equality also as a prescript for the burgher world. It invoked the "equality of the children of God" to infer civil equality, and partly even equality of property. Equality of nobleman and peasant, of patrician and privileged burgher, and the plebeian, abolition of compulsory labour, quitrents, taxes, privileges, and at least the most crying differences in property—those were demands advanced with more or less determination as natural implications of the early Christian doctrine. At the time when feudalism was at its zenith there was little to choose between this peasant-plebeian heresy of the Albigenses, for example, and the burgher opposition, but in the 14th and 15th centuries it developed into a clearly defined party opinion and usually took an independent stand alongside the heresy of the burghers. This was the relation of John Ball, preacher of Wat Tyler's rebellion in England, to the Wycliffe movement, and of the Taborites to the Calixtines in Bohemia. The Taborites even showed republican under a theocratic cloak, a view further developed by the plebeians in Germany in the fifteenth and early sixteenth century.

The fanaticism of mystically-minded sects, the Flagellants and Lollards,[1] etc., which continued the revolutionary tradition in times of suppression, seized upon this form of heresy.

At that time the plebeians were the only class that stood outside the existing official society. They had no access to either the feudal or the burgher association. They had

---

[1] *Flagellants* (or those who whipped themselves) were an ascetic religious sect widespread in Europe in the 13th to 15th centuries. The Flagellants propounded self-castigation as a means of expiating sins.

Lollards—a religious sect (originated in the 14th century) widespread in England. Bitterly opposed the Catholic Church. The Lollards were followers of Wycliffe, the English reformer, and drew more radical conclusions from his teaching. They adopted a religiously mystical stand against all feudal privileges. Many Lollards came from the people and the lower echelons of the priesthood. They took part in Tyler's rebellion of 1331 and were cruelly persecuted in the late 14th century. —*Ed.*

neither privileges nor property; they did not even have the kind of property the peasant or petty burgher had, which was heavily burdened with taxes. They were unpropertied and rightless in every respect; their living conditions never even brought them into direct contact with the existing institutions, which ignored them completely. They were a living symptom of the decay of the feudal and guild-burgher society, and at the same time the first precursors of the modern bourgeois society.

This explains why the plebeian opposition even then could not stop at fighting only feudalism and the privileged burghers; why, in fantasy at least, it reached beyond the then scarcely dawning modern bourgeois society; why, an absolutely propertyless faction, it questioned the institutions, views and conceptions common to all societies based on class antagonisms. In this respect, the chiliastic dream-visions[1] of early Christianity offered a very convenient starting point. On the other hand, this sally beyond both the present and even the future could be nothing but violent and fantastic, and of necessity fell back within the narrow limits set by the contemporary situation at the very first practical application of it. The attack on private property and demand for common ownership was bound to resolve into a primitive organisation of charity; vague Christian equality could at best resolve into civic "equality before the law" and elimination of all authority would finally culminate in the establishment of republican governments elected by the people. The anticipation of communism, nurtured by the imagination, became in reality an anticipation of modern bourgeois conditions.

This violent anticipation of coming historical developments, easily explained by the living conditions of the plebeians, is first recorded in *Germany*, with *Thomas Münzer*

---

[1] *Chiliasm* (from the Greek *chiliasmos*, derivative of *chilias*, a thousand)—a mystical religious doctrine that Christ would come to earth a second time and usher in a "millennium" of justice, equality and well-being. Chiliastic beliefs sprang up during the decay of slave society due to the unbearable oppression and suffering of the working people, who sought an outlet in fantastic visions of deliverance. These beliefs were widespread in early Christianity and continuously revived in the doctrines of the various medieval sects.—*Ed.*

and his party. The Taborites had a kind of chiliastic common ownership, but that was a purely military measure. Only in the teachings of Münzer did these communist notions express the aspirations of a real fraction of society. He formulated them with a certain definiteness, and they were observed since then in every great popular upheaval, until they gradually merged with the modern proletarian movement. It was all like the struggles of free peasants in the Middle Ages against the increasing feudal domination, which merged with the struggles of serfs and bondsmen for complete abolition of the feudal system.

While the first of the three large camps, the *conservative Catholic*, embraced all the elements interested in maintaining the existing conditions, i.e., the imperial authorities, the ecclesiastical and a section of the lay princes, the richer nobility, the prelates and the city patricians, the camp of *Lutheran* reforms, *moderate in the burgher manner*, attracted all the propertied elements of the opposition, the bulk of the lesser nobility, the burghers, and even a portion of the lay princes who hoped to enrich themselves through confiscation of church estates and wanted to seize the opportunity of gaining greater independence from the Empire. As to the peasants and plebeians, they formed a *revolutionary* party whose demands and doctrines were most clearly set out by Münzer.

Luther and Münzer each fully represented his party by his doctrine, as well as by his character, and actions.

From 1517 to 1525 *Luther* changed just as much as the present-day German constitutionalists did between 1846 and 1849, and as every bourgeois party which, placed for a time at the head of the movement, is overwhelmed by the plebeian proletarian party standing behind it.

When in 1517 Luther first opposed the dogmas and statutes of the Catholic Church his opposition was by no means of a definite character. Although it did not overstep the demands of the earlier burgher heresy, it did not, and could not, rule out any trend which went further. At that early stage all the opposition elements had to be united, the most resolute revolutionary energy displayed, and the sum of the existing heresies against the Catholic orthodoxy had to find a protagonist. In much the same way our liberal bourgeoisie of 1847 was still revolutionary, called itself socialist and communist, and clamoured for the emancipation of the working class. Luther's sturdy peasant nature asserted itself in the stormiest fashion in that first period of his activities. "If the raging madness (of the Roman churchmen) were to continue, it seems to me no better counsel and remedy could be found against it than that kings and princes apply force, arm themselves, attack those evil people who have poisoned the entire world, and put an end to this game once and for all, *with arms, not with words.* Since we punish thieves with the halter, murderers with the sword, and heretics with fire, why do we not turn on all those evil teachers of perdition, those popes, cardinals and bishops, and the entire swarm of the Roman Sodom *with arms in hand, and wash our hands in their blood?*"

But this revolutionary ardour was short-lived. Luther's lightning struck home. The entire German people was set in motion. On the one hand, peasants and plebeians saw the signal to revolt in his appeals against the clergy, and in his sermon of Christian freedom; on the other, he was joined by the moderate burghers and a large section of the lesser nobility. Even princes were drawn into the maelstrom. The former believed the day had come to wreak vengeance upon all their oppressors, the latter only wished to break the power of the clergy, the dependence upon Rome, to abolish the Catholic hierarchy and to enrich themselves on the confiscation of church property. The parties stood aloof of each other, and each had its spokesmen. Luther had to choose between them. He, the protégé of the Elector of Saxony, the revered professor of Wittenberg who had become powerful and famous overnight, the great man with his coterie of servile creatures and flatterers, did not hesitate for a single moment. He dropped the popular elements of the movement and took the side of the burghers, the nobility, and the princes. His appeals for a war of extermination against Rome resounded no more. Luther now preached *peaceful progress* and *passive resistance* (cf., for example, *To the Nobility of the German Nation,* 1520, etc.). Invited by Hutten to visit him and Sickingen in the castle of Ebern, where the nobility conspired against the clergy and the princes, Luther replied: "I do not wish the

Martin Luther

Gospel *defended by force and bloodshed.* The world was conquered by the Word, the Church is maintained by the Word, the Word will also put the Church back into its own, and Antichrist, who gained his own without violence, will fall without violence."

From this tendency, or, to be more exact, from this more definite delineation of Luther's policy, sprang that bartering and haggling over institutions and dogmas to be retained or reformed, that disgusting diplomatising, conciliating, intriguing and compromising, which resulted in the Augsburg Confession,[1] the finally importuned articles of a reformed burgher church. It was quite the same kind of petty bargaining as was recently repeated in political form *ad nauseam* at the German national assemblies, conciliatory gatherings, chambers of revision, and Erfurt parliaments. The Philistine nature of the official Reformation was most distinctly evident at these negotiations.

There were good reasons for Luther, henceforth the recognised representative of the burgher reform, to preach lawful progress. The bulk of the towns espoused the cause of moderate reform, the petty nobility became more and more devoted to it, and a section of the princes joined in, while another vacillated. Success was as good as won, at least in a large part of Germany. The remaining regions could not in the long run withstand the pressure of moderate opposition in the event of continued peaceful development. Any violent upheaval, meanwhile, was bound to bring the moderate party into conflict with the extremist plebeian and peasant party, to alienate the princes, the nobility, and many towns from the movement, leaving the alternative of either the burgher party being overshadowed by the peasants and plebeians or the entire movement being crushed

---

[1] *Augsburg Confession*—a statement of the Lutheran doctrine read to Emperor Charles V at the Imperial Diet in Augsburg; it adapted the burgher ideals of a cheap church (abolition of lavish rites, modification of the clerical hierarchy, etc.) to the interests of the princes. A prince was to replace the Pope at the head of the church. The Augsburg Confession was turned down by the Emperor. The war waged against him by princes who adopted the Lutheran Reformation ended in 1555 in the religious peace of Augsburg, which empowered the princes to determine the faith of their subjects at their own discretion.—*Ed.*

by Catholic restoration. There have been examples enough lately of how bourgeois parties, after gaining the slightest victory, seek to steer their way by means of lawful progress between the Scylla of revolution and the Charybdis of restoration.

Under the general social and political conditions prevailing at that time the results of every change were necessarily advantageous to the princes and inevitably increased their power. Thus it came about that the burgher reform fell the more completely under the control of the reformed princes, the more sharply it broke away from the plebeian and peasant elements. Luther himself became more and more their vassal, and the people knew perfectly well what they were doing when they accused him of having become, as the others, a flunkey of the princes, and when they stoned him in Orlamünde.

When the Peasant War broke out Luther tried to strike a mediatory pose in regions where the nobility and the princes were mostly Catholic. He resolutely attacked the authorities. He said they were to blame for the rebellion in view of their oppression; it was not the peasants, but God himself, who rose against them. Yet, on the other hand, he said, the revolt was ungodly and contrary to the Gospel. In conclusion, he called upon both parties to yield and reach a peaceful understanding.

But in spite of these well-meaning mediatory offers, the revolt spread swiftly, and even involved Protestant regions dominated by Lutheran princes, lords and towns, rapidly outgrowing the "circumspect" burgher reform. The most determined faction of the insurgents under Münzer made its headquarters in Luther's immediate proximity at Thuringia. A few more successes, and the whole of Germany would be in flames, Luther surrounded and perhaps piked as a traitor, and the burgher reform swept away by the tide of a peasant-plebeian revolution. There was no more time for circumspection. All the old animosities were forgotten in the face of the revolution. Compared with the hordes of peasants, the servants of the Roman Sodom were innocent lambs, sweet-tempered children of God. Burgher and prince, noble and clergyman, Luther and the Pope, all joined hands "against the murderous and plundering peasant hordes".[1] "They must be *knocked to pieces, strangled* and *stabbed, covertly* and *overtly*, by everyone who can, just as one must kill a *mad dog!*" Luther cried. "Therefore, dear sirs, help here, save there, stab, knock, strangle them everyone who can, and should you lose your life, bless you, no better death can you ever attain." There should be no false mercy for the peasant. Whoever hath pity on those whom God pities not, whom He wishes punished and destroyed, belongs among the rebels himself. Later the peasants would learn to thank God when they would have to give up one cow in order to enjoy the other in peace, and the princes would learn through the revolution the spirit of the mob that must be ruled by force only. "The wise man says: *cibus, onus et virga asino*.[2] The peasants must have nothing but chaff. They do not hearken to the Word, and are foolish, so they must hearken to the rod and the gun, and that serves them right. We must pray for them that they obey. Where they do not there should not be much mercy. *Let the guns roar among them*, or else they will do it a thousand times worse."

That was exactly what our late socialist and philanthropic bourgeoisie said when the proletariat claimed its share of the fruits of victory after the March events.

Luther had put a powerful weapon into the hands of the plebeian movement by translating the Bible. Through the Bible he contrasted the feudalised Christianity of his day with the moderate Christianity of the first centuries, and the decaying feudal society with a picture of a society that knew nothing of the ramified and artificial feudal hierarchy. The peasants had made extensive use of this instrument against the princes, the nobility, and the clergy. Now Luther turned it against the peasants, extracting from the Bible such a veritable hymn to the God-ordained authorities as no bootlicker of absolute monarchy had ever been able to extract. Princedom by the grace of God, resigned obedience, even serfdom, were sanctioned with the aid of the Bible. Not the peasant revolt alone, but Luther's own mutiny against religious and lay authority was thereby

---

[1] The title of a vicious pamphlet against the peasant movement published by Luther in May 1525, at the zenith of the Peasant War.—*Ed.*
[2] Latin for "food, pack, and lash to the ass".—*Ed.*

disavowed; not only the popular movement, but the burgher movement as well, were betrayed to the princes.

Need we name the bourgeois who recently gave us examples of such a disavowal of their own past?

Let us now compare the plebeian revolutionary, *Münzer,* with Luther, the burgher reformer.

Thomas Münzer was born in *Stolberg,* in the Harz, in 1498.[1] His father is said to have died on the scaffold, a victim of the obduracy of the Count of Stolberg. In his fifteenth year Münzer organised a secret union at the Halle school against the Archbishop of Magdeburg and the Roman Church in general. His learning in the theology of his time brought him an early doctor's degree and the position of chaplain in a Halle nunnery. Here he treated the church dogmas and rites with the greatest contempt. At mass he omitted the words of the transubstantiation, and, as Luther said, ate up the almighty gods unconsecrated. Medieval mystics, and particularly the chiliastic works of Joachim the Calabrese, were the main subject of his studies. The millennium and the Day of Judgment over the degenerated church and corrupted world propounded and described by that mystic, seemed to Münzer imminently close, what with the Reformation and the general unrest of his time. He preached in his neighbourhood with great success. In 1520 he went to Zwickau as the first evangelist preacher. There he found one of those fanatical chiliastic sects that continued their existence on the quiet in many localities, and whose momentary humility and detachment concealed the increasingly rampant opposition of the lowest strata of society to the prevailing conditions, and who were now, with the unrest growing, coming into the light of day ever more boldly and persistently. It was the sect of the Anabaptists[2] headed by Niklas *Storch.* They preached the approach of the Day of Judgment and of the millennium; they had "visions, transports, and the spirit of prophecy". They soon came into conflict with the Council of Zwickau. Münzer defend-

---

[1] This date was cited by Zimmermann in the first edition of his book. By a later verified date Thomas Münzer was born about 1490.—*Ed.*

[2] *Anabaptists*—a Christian sect so called because they repudiated infant baptism and demanded a second, adult baptism.—*Ed.*

ed them, though he never joined them unconditionally and would much rather have brought them under his own influence. The Council took drastic measures against them; they had to leave the town, and Münzer with them. This was at the close of 1521.

He went to Prague and sought to gain a foothold by joining the remnants of the Hussite movement. But his proclamation had the effect of compelling him to flee from Bohemia as well. In 1522 he became preacher at Allstedt in Thuringia. Here he started by reforming the cult. Even before Luther dared to go so far, he entirely abolished the Latin language and ordered the entire Bible, and not only the prescribed Sunday Gospels and epistles, to be read to the people. At the same time, he organised propaganda in his locality. People flocked to him from all directions, and Allstedt soon became the centre of the popular anti-priest movement of all Thuringia.

Münzer was as yet more theologian than anything else. He still directed his attacks almost exclusively against the priests. He did not, however, preach quiet debate and peaceful progress as Luther at that time, but continued Luther's earlier violent sermons, calling upon the princes of Saxony and the people to rise in arms against the Roman priests. "Does not Christ say, 'I came not to send peace, but a sword'? What must you (the princes of Saxony) do with that sword? Only one thing if you wish to be the servants of God, and that is to drive out and destroy the evil ones who stand in the way of the Gospel. Christ ordered very earnestly (Luke, 19, 27) 'bring hither mine enemies and slay them before me'. Do not give us any empty phrases that the power of God will do it without the aid of your sword, since then it would rust in its sheath.... Those who stand in the way of God's revelation must be destroyed mercilessly, as Hezekiah, Cyrus, Josiah, Daniel and Elias destroyed the priests of Baal, else the Christian Church will never come back to its source. We must uproot the weeds in God's vineyard at harvest time.... God said in the Fifth Book of Moses, 7, 'thou shalt not show mercy unto the idolaters, but ye shall destroy their altars, and break down their images and burn them with fire that I shall not be wroth at you'."

But these appeals to the princes were of no avail, whereas revolutionary sentiments among the people grew day by day. Münzer, whose ideas became more lucid and bolder, now broke resolutely away from the burgher Reformation, and henceforth became an outright political agitator.

His philosophico-theological doctrine attacked all the main points not only of Catholicism, but of Christianity generally. Under the cloak of Christianity he preached a kind of pantheism, which curiously resembled modern speculative contemplation[1] and at times even approached atheism. He repudiated the Bible both as the only and as the infallible revelation. The real and living revelation, he said, was reason, a revelation which existed and always exists among all peoples at all times. To hold up the Bible against reason, he maintained, was to kill the spirit with the letter, for the Holy Spirit of which the Bible speaks is not something that exists outside us—the Holy Spirit is our reason. Faith is nothing but reason come alive in man, and pagans could therefore also have faith. Through this faith, through reason come to life, man became godlike and blessed. Heaven is, therefore, nothing of another world and is to be sought in this life. It is the mission of believers to establish this Heaven, the kingdom of God, here on earth. Just as there is no Heaven in the beyond, there is also no Hell and no damnation. Similarly, there is no devil but man's evil lusts and greed. Christ was a man, as we are, a prophet and a teacher, and his supper is a plain meal of commemoration wherein bread and wine are consumed without any mystic garnish.

Münzer preached these doctrines mostly cloaked in the same Christian phraseology, behind which the new philosophy had to hide for some time. But the arch-heretical fundamental idea is easily discerned in all his writings, and he obviously took the biblical cloak much less in earnest than many a disciple of Hegel does in modern times. Yet three hundred years separate Münzer from modern philosophy.

Münzer's political doctrine followed his revolutionary re-

---

[1] Engels refers to the views of the German idealist philosopher Strauss and other Young Hegelians who treated questions of religion from a pantheist standpoint in their early writings.—*Ed.*

ligious conceptions very closely, and just as his theology overstepped the current conceptions of his time, so his political doctrine overstepped the directly prevailing social and political conditions. Just as Münzer's religious philosophy approached atheism, so his political programme approached communism, and even on the eve of the February Revolution more than one present-day communist sect lacked as comprehensive a theoretical arsenal as was "Münzer's" in the sixteenth century. This programme, no more of a compilation of the demands of the plebeians of that day than a visionary anticipation of the conditions for the emancipation of the proletarian element that had scarcely begun to develop among the plebeians—this programme demanded the immediate establishment of the kingdom of God, of the prophesied millennium, by restoring the church to its original status and abolishing all the institutions that conflicted with this allegedly early-Christian, but in fact very novel church. By the kingdom of God Münzer meant a society without class differences, private property and a state authority independent of, and foreign to, the members of society. All the existing authorities, insofar as they refused to submit and join the revolution, were to be overthrown, all work and all property shared in common, and complete equality introduced. A union was to be established to realise all this, and not only throughout Germany, but throughout all Christendom. Princes and lords would be invited to join, and should they refuse, the union was to take up arms and overthrow or kill them at the first opportunity.

Münzer set to work at once to organise the union. His sermons became still more militant and revolutionary. He thundered forth against the princes, the nobility and the patricians with a passion that equalled the fervour of his attacks upon the clergy. He depicted the prevailing oppression in burning colours and countered it with his dream-vision of the millennium of social republican equality. He published one revolutionary pamphlet after another, and sent emissaries in all directions, while personally organising the union in Allstedt and its vicinity.

The first fruit of this propaganda was the destruction of St. Mary's Chapel in Mellerbach near Allstedt, according to

Thomas Münzer

the command of the Bible (Deut. 7, 6): "Ye shall destroy their altars, and dash in pieces their pillars, and burn their graven images with fire." The princes of Saxony came in person to Allstedt to quell the unrest and bid Münzer come to the castle. There he delivered a sermon the like of which they had not heard from Luther, "that easy-living flesh of Wittenberg", as Münzer called him. Münzer maintained that ungodly rulers, especially priests and monks, who treated the Gospel as heresy, should be killed, and referred to the New Testament for confirmation. The ungodly had no right to live save by the mercy of God's elect. If the princes did not exterminate the ungodly, God would take their sword from them, *because the entire community had the power of the sword*. The princes and lords are the prime movers of usury, thievery and robbery; they take all creatures into their private possession—the fish in the water, the birds in the air, and the plants in the soil—and still preach to the poor the commandment, "Thou shalt not steal," while they themselves take everything they find, rob and oppress the peasant and the artisan. But if one of the latter commits the slightest transgression, he has to hang, and Dr. Lügner[1] says to all this: Amen. "The masters themselves are to blame that the poor man becomes their enemy. If they do not remove the causes of the upheaval, how can things go well in the long run? Oh, dear sirs, how the Lord will smite these old pots with an iron rod! But for saying so, I am regarded a rebel. So be it!" (Cf. Zimmermann's *Bauernkrieg*, II, p. 75).

Münzer had the sermon printed. His Allstedt printer was punished by Duke Johann of Saxony with banishment, while Münzer's writings were to be censored from then on by the ducal government in Weimar. But he paid no heed to this order. He hastened to publish a highly inciting paper[2] in the imperial city of Mühlhausen, wherein he called on the people "to widen the hole so that all the world may see

---

[1] Münzer refers to Luther; a play on the word "Lügner", the German for "liar".—*Ed.*

[2] Engels alludes to Münzer's pamphlet, *Open Denial of the False Belief of the Godless World on the Testimony of the Gospel of Luke, Presented to Miserable and Pitiful Christendom in Memory of Its Error*, which appeared in Mühlhausen in 1524.—*Ed.*

and understand who our great personages are that have blasphemously turned our Lord into a painted manikin". It ended with the following words: "All the world must suffer a big jolt. There will be such a game that the ungodly will be thrown off their seats, and the downtrodden will rise." Thomas Münzer, "the man with the hammer", wrote the following motto on the title page: "Beware, I have put my words into the mouth, I have put you over the people and over the Empire that thou mayest uproot, destroy, scatter and overthrow, and that thou mayest build and plant. A wall of iron against the kings, princes, priests, and against the people hath been erected. Let them fight, for victory will wondrously lead to the perdition of the strong and godless tyrants."[1]

Münzer's breach with Luther and his party had taken place long before that. Luther had to accept some of the church reforms which Münzer had introduced without consulting him. He watched Münzer's activities with a moderate reformer's nettled mistrust of a more energetic, farther-aiming party. Already in the spring of 1525, in a letter to Melanchthon, that model of a hectic stay-at-home Philistine, Münzer wrote that he and Luther did not understand the movement at all. He said they sought to choke it by the letter of the Bible, and that their doctrine was worm-eaten. "Dear brethren," he wrote, "cease your procrastination and vacillation. It is time, summer is knocking at the door. Do not keep friendship with the ungodly who hinder the Word from working its full force. Do not flatter your princes, or you may perish with them. Ye tender bookish scholars, do not be wroth, for I can do nothing to change it."

Luther had more than once challenged Münzer to an open debate. The latter, however, always ready to take up the battle before the people, had not the least desire to let himself in for a theological squabble before the partisan public of Wittenberg University. He did not wish "to bring the testimony of the Spirit exclusively before the high

---

[1] In the epigraph to his essay Münzer paraphrases words from the Book of the Prophet Jeremiah (Old Testament), infusing it with revolutionary purport.—*Ed.*

school of learning". If Luther were sincere, he should use his influence to stop the chicaneries against his, Münzer's printer, and lift the censorship so that their controversy might be freely fought in the press.

But now, when Münzer's above-mentioned revolutionary brochure appeared, Luther denounced him publicly. In his *Letter to the Princes of Saxony Against the Rebellious Spirit* he declared Münzer to be an instrument of Satan and demanded of the princes to intervene and drive the instigators of the upheaval out of the country, since they did not confine themselves to preaching their evil doctrine but incited to insurrection, to violent action against the authorities.

On August 1, Münzer was compelled to appear before the princes in the castle of Weimar on the charge of incitement to mutiny. Highly compromising facts were available against him; they were on the scent of his secret union; his hand was detected in the societies of the miners and the peasants. He was threatened with banishment. No sooner had he returned to Allstedt than he learned that Duke Georg of Saxony demanded his extradition. Union letters in his handwriting had been intercepted, wherein he called Georg's subjects to armed resistance against the enemies of the Gospel. The Council would have extradited him, had he not left the town.

In the meantime, the growing unrest among the peasants and plebeians had made it incomparably easier for Münzer to carry on his propaganda. In the Anabaptists he found invaluable agents for that purpose. This sect, which had no positive dogmas, held together only by its common opposition to all ruling classes and by the common symbol of the second baptism, ascetic in their mode of living, untiring, fanatical and intrepid in carrying on propaganda, had grouped itself more and more closely around Münzer. Made homeless by persecutions, its members wandered all over Germany and carried word everywhere of the new teaching, in which Münzer had made their own demands and wishes clear to them. Countless Anabaptists were put on the rack, burned or otherwise executed, but the courage and endurance of these emissaries were unshakeable, and the success of their activities amid the rapidly growing unrest was enormous. Thus, after his flight from Thuringia, Münzer found the ground prepared wherever he turned.

Near Nuremberg, where Münzer went first, a peasant revolt had been nipped in the bud a month before.[1] Münzer conducted his propaganda surreptitiously; people soon appeared who defended his most audacious theological propositions on the non-obligatory nature of the Bible and the meaninglessness of sacraments, who declared Christ a mere man and the power of the lay authorities ungodly. "There is Satan stalking, the Spirit of Allstedt!" Luther exclaimed. In Nuremberg Münzer printed his reply to Luther.[2] He accused him of flattering the princes and supporting the reactionary party through his insipid moderation. But the people would free themselves all the same, he wrote, and it would go with Dr. Luther as with a captive fox. The Council ordered the paper confiscated, and Münzer had to leave Nuremberg.

Now he went across Swabia to Alsace, then to Switzerland, and then back to the Upper Black Forest, where an insurrection had broken out several months before, largely precipitated by his Anabaptist emissaries. This propaganda tour of Münzer's had unquestionably and substantially contributed to the establishment of the people's party, to the clear formulation of its demands and to the final general outbreak of the insurrection in April 1525. It was through this trip that the dual effect of Münzer's activities became particularly apparent—on the one hand, on the people, whom he addressed in the only language they could then comprehend, that of religious prophecy; and, on the other hand, on the initiated, to whom he could disclose his ultimate aims. Even before his journey he had assembled in Thuringia a circle of resolute men from among the people

---

[1] According to later information Münzer first went to the imperial town of Mühlhausen, from where he was banished in September 1524 for taking part in disturbances among the city poor. From Mühlhausen Münzer came to Nuremberg.—*Ed.*

[2] Münzer's pointed reply to Luther was entitled *A Well-Grounded Defence and Reply to the Godless, Easy-Living Flesh of Wittenberg, Which Has Pitifully Sullied Unhappy Christianity Through Shameless Distortions of the Holy Scripture.—Ed.*

and the lesser clergy, whom he had put at the head of his secret society. Now he became the soul of the entire revolutionary movement in Southwestern Germany, organised ties between Saxony and Thuringia through Franconia and Swabia up to Alsace and the Swiss border, and counted such South-German agitators as Hubmaier of Waldshut, Conrad Grebel of Zürich, Franz Rabmann of Griessen, Schappeler of Memmingen, Jakob Wehe of Leipheim, and Dr. Mantel in Stuttgart, who were mostly revolutionary priests, among his disciples and the heads of the union. He himself stayed mostly in Griessen on the Schaffhausen border, journeying from there across the Hegau, Klettgau, etc. The bloody persecutions undertaken by the alarmed princes and lords everywhere against this new plebeian heresy, contributed not a little to fanning the spirit of rebellion and consolidating the ranks of the union. In this way Münzer conducted his agitation for about five months in Upper Germany, and returned to Thuringia when the outbreak of the conspiracy was near at hand, because he wished to lead the movement personally. There we shall find him later.

We shall see how truly the character and behaviour of the two party leaders reflected the attitude of their respective parties, how Luther's indecision and fear of the movement, which was assuming serious proportions, and his cowardly servility to the princes, fully corresponded to the hesitant and ambiguous policy of the burghers, and how Münzer's revolutionary energy and resolution was reproduced among the most advanced section of the plebeians and peasants. The only difference was that while Luther confined himself to expressing the conceptions and wishes of the majority of his class and thereby won an extremely cheap popularity among it, Münzer, on the contrary, went far beyond the immediate ideas and demands of the plebeians and peasants, and organised a party of the élite of the then existing revolutionary elements, which, inasmuch as it shared his ideas and energy, always remained only a small minority of the insurgent masses.

III

The first signs of a budding revolutionary spirit appeared among the German peasants about fifty years after the suppression of the Hussite movement.*

In 1476 the first peasant conspiracy occurred in the bishopric of Würzburg, a land impoverished by the Hussite wars, "by bad government, manifold taxes, payments, feuds, enmity, war, fire, murder, prison, and the like",[1] and continually and shamelessly plundered by bishops, priests and the nobility. A young shepherd and musician, *Hans Böheim of Niklashausen*, also called the Drum-Beater and *Hans the Piper*, suddenly appeared in the Tauber valley in the role of prophet. He declared that he had had a vision of the Virgin Mary, that she had commanded him to burn his drum, to cease serving the dance and sinful sensuality, and to exhort the people to do penance. Everyone should purge himself of sin and the vain lusts of the world, forsake all adornments and embellishments, and make a pilgrimage to the Madonna of Niklashausen to obtain forgiveness.

Already among these precursors of the movement we find an asceticism typical of all medieval uprisings tinged with religion, and, in modern times, of the early stages of every proletarian movement. This ascetic austerity of morals, this demand to forsake all joys of life and all entertainments, opposes the ruling classes with the principle of Spartan equality, on the one hand, and is, on the other, a necessary transition stage, without which the lowest stratum of society can never set itself in motion. In order to develop their revolutionary energy, to become conscious of their own hostile attitude towards all other elements of society, to concentrate themselves as a class, the lower strata of society must begin by stripping themselves of everything that could reconcile them with the existing social system; they must renounce the few pleasures that make their grievous

---

* In our chronology we are following the data given by Zimmermann, upon which we are obliged to rely in the absence of adequate sources abroad and which are quite satisfactory for the purposes of the present work. *Footnote by Engels to the 1850 edition.*

[1] Engels quotes an extract from a 15th-century manuscript preserved in the Würzburg archive and cited by Zimmermann.—*Ed.*

position in the least tolerable for the moment, and of which even the severest oppression could not deprive them. This *plebeian and proletarian asceticism* differs both in its wild fanatical form and in its essence from the bourgeois asceticism of the Lutheran burgher morality and of the English Puritans (as distinct from the Independents and the more radical sects), whose entire secret lay in *bourgeois thrift*. It stands to reason that this plebeian-proletarian asceticism gradually sheds its revolutionary nature when the development of modern productive forces infinitely multiplies the luxuries, thus rendering Spartan equality superfluous, and as the position of the proletariat in society, and thereby the proletariat itself, become ever more revolutionary. This asceticism disappears gradually from among the masses, and in the sects, which relied upon it, it degenerates either into bourgeois parsimony or into a high-sounding virtuousness which, in practice, also comes down to a Philistine, or guild-artisan, niggardliness. Besides, renunciation of pleasures need hardly be preached to the proletariat for the simple reason that it has almost nothing more to renounce.

Hans the Piper's call to penitence found a ready response. All the prophets of rebellion started with appeals against sin, and, indeed, only a violent exertion, a sudden renunciation of all this habitual mode of existence could bring this disunited, widely scattered, sparsely sown peasant species, raised in blind submission, into concerted motion. The pilgrimages to Niklashausen began and rapidly increased, and the more massive the stream of pilgrims, the more openly the young rebel spoke out his plans. The Madonna of Niklashausen had told him, he preached, that henceforth there should be neither king nor prince, neither Pope nor any other ecclesiastic or lay authority. Each should be a brother to the other and win his bread by the toil of his own hands, and that none should have more than his neighbour. All tributes, ground rents, services, tolls, taxes, and other payments and duties should be forever abolished, and forest, water and pasture should everywhere be free.

The people received this new gospel with joy. The fame of the prophet, "the message of our Lady", spread far and wide; pilgrim throngs flocked to him from Odenwald, from the Main, Kocher and Jagst, even from Bavaria and Swabia, and from the Rhine. Miracles were recounted, said to have been performed by the Piper; people fell to their knees before him, praying to him as to a saint, and then fought for the tufts from his cap for relics or amulets. In vain did the priests speak against him, denouncing his visions as the devil's delusions and his miracles as diabolic swindles. The mass of the believers increased inordinately, a revolutionary sect began to take shape, the Sunday sermons of the rebel shepherd drew gatherings of 40,000 and more to Niklashausen.

Hans the Piper preached to the masses for a number of months, but he did not intend to confine himself to preaching. He had secret connections with the pastor of Niklashausen and with two knights, Kunz von Thunfeld and his son, who held to the new teaching and were to become the military leaders of the planned insurrection. Finally, on the Sunday before the day of St. Kilian, when his power appeared to be great enough, the shepherd gave the signal. "And now go home," he closed his sermon, "and weigh in your mind what our holiest Lady has announced to you, and on the coming Saturday leave your wives and children and old men at home, and you, men, come back to Niklashausen on the day of St. Margaret, which is next Saturday, and bring your brothers and friends, as many as they may be. Do not come with pilgrims' staves, however, but with armour and arms, a candle in one hand, and a sword, pike or halberd in the other, and the Holy Virgin will then tell you what she wishes you to do."

But before the peasants arrived in their numbers, the bishop's horsemen seized the rebel prophet at night and brought him to the castle of Würzburg. On the appointed day almost 34,000 armed peasants appeared, but the news crushed them. Most of them went home, while the initiated kept about 16,000 together, with whom they marched to the castle under the leadership of Kunz von Thunfeld and his son Michael. The bishop persuaded them with promises to turn back, but no sooner had they begun to disperse than they were attacked by the bishop's horsemen, and many of them taken captive. Two were decapitated, and Hans the Piper was burned at the stake. Kunz von Thunfeld escaped and was allowed to return only after ceding all his estates to the bishopric. The pilgrimages to Niklashausen continued for some time, but were finally also suppressed.

After this initial attempt, Germany remained quiet for some time. Only towards the close of the century new peasant revolts and conspiracies broke out.

We shall pass over the Dutch peasant revolt of 1491 and 1492, which was suppressed by Duke Albrecht of Saxony in the battle of Heemskerk, the simultaneous peasant revolt in the Abbey of Kempten in Upper Swabia, and the Frisian revolt under Syaard Aylva, about 1497, which was also suppressed by Albrecht of Saxony. These revolts were partly too far from the scene of the Peasant War proper, and partly uprisings of hitherto free peasants against the attempt to force feudalism upon them. We pass on to the two great conspiracies which laid the ground for the Peasant War: the *Bundschuh* and the *Poor Konrad*.

The rise in prices that had caused the peasant revolt in the Netherlands in 1493 brought about in Alsace a secret union of peasants and plebeians with a sprinkling of the purely burgher opposition, and with a certain amount of sympathy even among the lesser nobility. The seat of the union was in the region of Schlettstadt, Sulz, Dambach, Rosheim, Scherweiler, etc. The conspirators wanted to plunder and exterminate Jews, whose usury then, as now, sucked dry the peasants of Alsace, and demanded the proclamation of a jubilee year to cancel all debts, lift duties, tolls and other burdens, abolish the ecclesiastical and Rottweil (imperial) court, the right of the Estates to ratify taxes, to reduce the priests' prebend to fifty or sixty guilders, abolish the auricular confession, and establish in the communities courts elected by the communities themselves. As soon as they became strong enough the conspirators planned to overpower the stronghold of Schlettstadt, to confiscate the treasuries of the monasteries and the town and from there to arouse the whole of Alsace. The banner of the Union, which was to be unfurled at the start of the uprising, depicted a peasant's clog with long leather strings, the so-called *Bundschuh*, which served peasant conspiracies as an emblem and name in the following twenty years.

The conspirators were wont to hold their meetings at night on the lonesome Hunger Hill. Initiation into the

Title page of a leaflet directed against the peasants who have revolted

Bundschuh involved the most mysterious of ceremonies and the severest threats of punishment for betrayal. But the affair got abroad about Easter Week of 1493, the time appointed for the attack on Schlettstadt. The authorities stepped in immediately. Many of the conspirators were arrested and tortured, some were quartered or decapitated, and others had their hands or fingers cut off and were driven out of the country. A great many fled to Switzerland.

The Bundschuh, however, was far from crushed by these first blows. On the contrary, it continued in secret and the numerous fugitives, scattered all over Switzerland and Southern Germany, became as many emissaries. Men found the same oppression everywhere and, consequently, the same inclination to revolt. They propagated the Bundschuh throughout the present-day Baden. The tenacity and stamina with which the peasants of Upper Germany conspired for about thirty years after 1493, with which they surmounted all the obstacles arising from their scattered way of life on the road to a larger, more centralised organisation, and with which they renewed their conspiracies over and over again after countless dispersions, defeats, and executions of their leaders, until an opportunity came at last for a mass uprising—this tenacity is really admirable.

In 1502 there were signs of a secret movement among the peasants of the bishopric of Speyer, which at that time also embraced the locality of Bruchsal. The Bundschuh had reorganised itself there with really considerable success. About 7,000 men belonged to the society, whose centre was in Untergrombach, between Bruchsal and Weingarten, and whose ramifications reached down the Rhine to the Main, and up to the Margraviate of Baden. Its articles said: neither ground rent nor tithe, neither tax nor toll are to be paid any longer to the princes, the nobility, or the clergy; serfdom is to be abolished; the monasteries and other *church estates are to be confiscated and divided among the people, and no other ruler is to be recognised save the Emperor.*

Here we find for the first time expressed by peasants the two demands of secularising church estates in favour of the people, and of a united and indivisible German monarchy—the two demands which will henceforth be advocated regularly by the more advanced peasants and plebeians, until Thomas Münzer changes *distribution* of church estates to *confiscation* and conversion into *commonly-owned property*, and a united German *Empire* to a united and indivisible *republic*.

The revived Bundschuh, like the old, had its own secret meeting place, its oath of silence, its initiation ceremonies, and its union banner with the legend, "Nothing but God's Justice!" Its plan of action was similar to that of the Alsatian union. Bruchsal, most of whose inhabitants belonged to the Bundschuh, was to be overpowered and a Bundschuh army organised there and sent into the surrounding principalities as an itinerant meeting point.

The plan was betrayed by a clergyman who learned of it from one of the conspirators in the confessional. The authorities instantly took countermeasures. How widespread the Bundschuh had become is evident from the terror that seized the various imperial estates in Alsace and in the Swabian League.[1] Troops were concentrated, and mass arrests were made. Emperor Maximilian, "last of the knights", issued a bloodthirsty punitive decree against the audacious peasant undertaking. Throngs of peasants assembled here and there and offered armed resistance, but the isolated peasant troops could not hold out for long. Some of the conspirators were executed, others escaped; but secrecy was so well preserved that the majority, even the leaders, remained unmolested in their own localities and in the possessions of the neighbouring lords.

After this new defeat there followed a prolonged period of apparent calm in the class struggle. But work went on underground. In the first years of the sixteenth century *Poor Konrad* appeared in Swabia, evidently with the support of the scattered members of the Bundschuh. In the Black Forest the Bundschuh continued in small isolated groups

---

[1] *Swabian League* of princes, noblemen and patricians of the imperial towns of Southwestern Germany, organised in 1488. Its chief purpose was to combat the peasant and plebeian movement. The South- and West-German princes who headed this reactionary League, also hoped to establish their oligarchic rule through it over Germany. The League had its own administrative and juridical bodies, and an army. It fell apart in 1534 due to internal squabbles.—*Ed.*

until, ten years later, an energetic peasant leader succeeded in gathering the various isolated threads into a major conspiracy. Both conspiracies became public, one after the other, in the restless years of 1513-15, in which the Swiss, Hungarian and Slovenian peasants rose simultaneously in a series of major insurrections.

The man who revived the Upper Rhine Bundschuh was *Joss Fritz* of Untergrombach, a fugitive of the conspiracy of 1502, a former soldier, and in all respects an outstanding figure. After his flight he stayed in various localities between Lake of Constance and the Black Forest, and finally settled in Lehen near Freiburg in Breisgau, where he even became a forester. Most interesting facts are contained in the court records about the manner in which he reorganised the Bundschuh from that vantage point and how ingeniously he recruited people of different kinds. The diplomatic talent and tireless energy of this model conspirator succeeded in enrolling a great number of people of various classes into the Bundschuh: knights, priests, burghers, plebeians and peasants, and it appears almost certain that he even organised several more or less sharply divided grades of the conspiracy. All serviceable elements were utilised with the greatest circumspection and skill. Apart from the more initiated emissaries who traversed the country in various disguises, vagrants and beggars were employed for subordinate missions. Joss stood in direct contact with the beggar kings, and through them held the numerous vagabond population in the palm of his hand. The beggar kings played a considerable role in his conspiracy. They were very bizarre figures: one roamed the country with a girl whose seemingly wounded feet were his pretext for begging; he had more than eight insignia on his hat—the Fourteen Deliverers, St. Ottilie, Our Mother in Heaven, etc., and, besides, he wore a long red beard and carried a big knotty stick with a dagger and pike. Another, who begged in the name of St. Velten, had spices and wormseeds for sale, and wore a long steel-coloured coat, a red barret with the Baby of Trient attached to it, a sword at his side, and many knives and a dagger in his girdle. Others had bleeding wounds, which they inflicted upon themselves, and their attire was also picturesque. There were at least ten of them, and for the price of two thousand guilders they were simultaneously to set aflame Alsace, the Margraviate of Baden, and Breisgau, and to put themselves, with at least 2,000 of their kind, under the command of Georg Schneider, a former captain of the lansquenets, on the day of the Zabern parish fair in Rosen, in order to take possession of that town. A courier service from station to station was established by members of the Bundschuh, and Joss Fritz and his chief emissary, Stoffel of Freiburg, rode continually from place to place to stage nocturnal military reviews of neophytes. The court records offer ample evidence of the spread of the Bundschuh in the Upper Rhine and Black Forest regions. They contain countless names and descriptions of members from the various localities of that region—most of them journeymen, then peasants and innkeepers, a few nobles, priests (like the one from Lehen), and breadless lansquenets. This composition of the Bundschuh indicates the more developed character of the society under Joss Fritz. The urban plebeian element was asserting itself more and more. The ramifications of the conspiracy spread throughout Alsace, the present-day Baden, up to Württemberg, and the Main. From time to time large gatherings were held on secluded mountains such as the Kniebis, etc., to discuss the affairs of the society. The meetings of the chiefs, in which local members and delegates of remoter localities often participated, took place on the Hartmatte near Lehen, and it was there that the fourteen articles of the Bundschuh were adopted. The articles agreed upon were: no master outside the Emperor, and (according to some) the Pope; abolition of the Rottweil imperial court and restriction of the church court to religious affairs; abolition of interest after it had been paid for so long that it equalled the capital; top interest rate of 5 per cent; freedom of hunting, fishing, pasture, and wood cutting; restriction of priests to each one prebend; confiscation of all church estates and monastery treasures for the Bundschuh war chest; abolition of all inequitable taxes and tolls; eternal peace in all Christendom; determined action against all opponents of the Bundschuh; Bundschuh taxes; seizure of a strong town, such as Freiburg, to serve as Bundschuh headquarters; negotiations with the Emperor as soon as the Bundschuh throngs are gathered, and with Switzerland in case the Emperor declines. It is evident that the demands of the peasants and plebeians were becoming more definite and firm, and that, on the other hand, concessions had also to be made in the same measure to the moderate and timid.

The blow was to be struck about autumn 1513. Only a Bundschuh banner was lacking, and Joss Fritz went to Heilbronn to have it painted. Besides all sorts of emblems and pictures, it bore the peasant's clog emblem and the legend, "God help thy divine justice". While he was away a premature attempt was made to overwhelm Freiburg, which was discovered. Some indiscretions in the conduct of propaganda put the Council of Freiburg and the Margrave of Baden on its scent, and the betrayal by two conspirators completed the series of disclosures. The Margrave, the Council of Freiburg, and the imperial government at Ensisheim[1] instantly sent spies and soldiers; a number of Bundschuh members were arrested, tortured and executed. But again the majority escaped, Joss Fritz among them. This time the Swiss government sternly persecuted the fugitives, and even executed many of them. However, it had just as little success as its neighbours in preventing the greater part of the fugitives from keeping continually in the vicinity of their former homes and even returning to them after some time. The Alsace government in Ensisheim acted more cruelly than the others. It ordered very many to be decapitated, broken on the wheel, and quartered. Joss Fritz himself kept mainly to the Swiss bank of the Rhine, but often crossed to the Black Forest, without ever being apprehended.

Why this time the Swiss made common cause against the Bundschuh with the neighbouring governments is apparent from the peasant revolt that broke out the following year, 1514, in Berne, Solothurn and Lucerne, and resulted in a purge of the aristocratic governments and the patriciate generally. The peasants also won certain privileges for themselves. The success of the local Swiss revolts was simply due to the fact that there was even less centralisation

---

[1] i.e., the government of the vicegerent of the Austrian Hapsburgs in Upper Alsace and Breisgau.—*Ed.*

in Switzerland than in Germany. In 1525 the peasants managed to dispose of their local lords everywhere, but succumbed to the organised armies of the princes, and it was these latter that Switzerland did not have.

Simultaneously with the Bundschuh in Baden, and apparently in direct association with it, a second conspiracy was formed in Württemberg. Documents indicate that it had existed since 1503, but since the name Bundschuh became too dangerous after the setback of the Untergrombach conspirators, it adopted the name *Poor Konrad*. Its seat was the valley of the Rems at the foot of the mountain of Hohenstaufen. Its existence was for long no secret, at least to the people. The unscrupulous oppression of Duke Ulrich's government and a number of famine years, which contributed greatly to the outbreak of the movements of 1513 and 1514, had increased the number of conspirators. The newly imposed taxes on wine, meat and bread, and a capital tax of one pfennig yearly for every guilder, provoked the uprising. The town of Schorndorf, where the heads of the complot met in the house of a cutler named Kaspar Pregizer, was to be seized first. In the spring of 1514, the rebellion broke out. Three thousand, and according to some, five thousand peasants gathered before the town, but were persuaded by the amicable promises of the Duke's officers to withdraw. Duke Ulrich, who had agreed to abolish the new taxes, arrived posthaste with eighty horsemen to find everything quiet in consequence of the promise. He promised to convene a Diet to examine all complaints. But the chiefs of the society knew very well that Ulrich sought only to keep the people quiet until he recruited and concentrated enough troops to be able to break his word and collect the taxes by force. From Kaspar Pregizer's house, "Poor Konrad's chancery", they issued a call for a society congress, and sent emissaries in all directions. The success of the first uprising in the Rems valley had everywhere stimulated the movement among the people. The appeals and the emissaries found a favourable response, and the congress held in Untertürkheim on May 28 was attended by numerous representatives from all parts of Württemberg. It was decided to proceed at once with propaganda and to strike in the Rems valley at the first opportunity, in order to spread the uprising from that point in every direction. While Bantelhans of Dettingen, a former soldier, and Singerhans of Würtingen, an esteemed peasant, were bringing the Swabian Alb into the society, the uprising broke out on every side. Though Singerhans was attacked and seized, the towns of Backnang, Winnenden, and Markgröningen fell into the hands of the peasants who had joined forces with the plebeians, and the entire area from Weinsberg to Blaubeuren, and from there to the border of Baden, was in open revolt. Ulrich was compelled to yield. However, while he called the Diet for June 25, he wrote to the surrounding princes and free towns asking for aid against the uprising, which, he said, threatened all princes, authorities and nobles in the Empire, and which "bore an uncommon resemblance to the Bundschuh".

In the meantime, the Diet, i.e., the deputies of the towns, and many delegates of the peasants who also demanded seats in the Diet, came together as early as June 18 in Stuttgart. The prelates had not yet arrived. The knights had not been invited. The city opposition of Stuttgart, as well as two threatening peasant throngs at Leonberg and in the Rems valley, supported the demands of the peasants. Their delegates were admitted, and it was decided to depose and punish the three hated councillors of the Duke—Lamparter, Thumb and Lorcher, appoint for the Duke a council of four knights, four burghers and four peasants, to grant him a fixed civil allowance, and to confiscate the monasteries and endowments in favour of the State treasury.

Duke Ulrich countered these revolutionary decisions with a coup d'état. On June 21 he rode with his knights and councillors to Tübingen, where he was followed by the prelates, ordered the burghers to come there as well, which they did, and there continued the Diet session without the peasants. The burghers, confronted with military terror, betrayed their peasant allies. On July 8 the Tübingen agreement came into being, which imposed on the country almost a million of the Duke's debts, laid some restrictions on the Duke which he never observed, and disposed of the peasants with a few meagre general phrases and a very definite penal law against insurrection and association. Naturally, nothing was said any more about peasant representation in the Diet. The peasantry cried treason, but the Duke, who had acquired new credit after his debts were taken over by the Estates, soon gathered troops, and his neighbours, particularly the Elector Palatine, also sent him military aid. The Tübingen agreement was thus accepted all over the country towards the end of July, and a new oath taken. In the Rems valley alone, Poor Konrad offered resistance. The Duke, who again rode there in person, was almost killed. A peasant camp was set up on the mountain of Kappel. But as the affair dragged on, most of the insurgents dispersed for lack of food, and the rest also went home after an ambiguous agreement with some of the Diet deputies. In the meantime, Ulrich, his army strengthened with companies willingly placed at his service by the towns, which, having attained their demands, turned fanatically against the peasants, attacked the Rems valley in spite of the agreement and plundered its towns and villages. Sixteen hundred peasants were taken prisoner, sixteen of them instantly decapitated, and the rest made to pay heavy fines to Ulrich's treasury. Many remained in prison for a long time. A number of penal laws were enacted against a revival of the society, against all gatherings of peasants, and the nobility of Swabia formed a special league for the suppression of all attempts at insurrection. The top leaders of Poor Konrad had meanwhile succeeded in escaping to Switzerland, whence after a few years the bulk of them returned home, mostly singly.

At the time of the Württemberg movement, signs of new Bundschuh activities were observed in Breisgau and in the Margraviate of Baden. In June, an insurrection was attempted near Bühl, but it was quickly throttled by Margrave Philip, and its leader, Gugel-Bastian, was seized in Freiburg and beheaded.

In the spring of the same year, 1514, a general peasant war broke out in *Hungary*. A crusade against the Turks was preached, and freedom was promised, as usual, to the serfs and bondsmen who would join it. About 60,000 gathered under the command of Georg Dózsa, a Székler,[1] who

---

[1] *Székler*—a Magyar of Eastern and Northeastern Transylvania.—*Ed.*

had distinguished himself in previous Turkish wars and attained nobility. The Hungarian knights and magnates, however, looked with disfavour upon the crusade, which threatened to deprive them of their property and bondsmen. They overtook isolated peasant groups, took back their serfs by force, and mistreated them. When this reached the ears of the army of crusaders the fury of the oppressed peasants broke loose. Two of the most enthusiastic advocates of the crusade, Laurentius Mészéros and Barnabás, fanned the hatred against the nobility in the army by their revolutionary speeches. Dózsa himself was as angered as his troops with the treacherous nobility. The army of crusaders became an army of revolution and Dózsa put himself at the head of the new movement.

He camped with his peasants in the Rákos field near Pest. Clashes of the nobility with the people in the surrounding villages and the suburbs of Pest opened the hostilities. It soon came to skirmishes, and then to Sicilian Vespers[1] for all the noblemen who fell into the hands of the peasants, and to the destruction by fire of all the castles in the vicinity. The court made its threats in vain. After the first acts of popular justice against the nobility had been accomplished, under the walls of the capital, Dózsa proceeded with further operations. He divided his army into five columns. Two were sent to the mountains of Upper Hungary to rouse the populace and exterminate the nobility. The third, under Ambros Száleresi, a citizen of Pest, remained on the Rákos to watch the capital, while the fourth and fifth were led by Dózsa and his brother Gregor against Szegedin.

In the meantime, the nobility gathered in Pest, and called to its aid Johann Zápolya, the *voivode* of Transylvania. Joined by the burghers of Budapest, they attacked and annihilated the army on the Rákos, after Száleresi and the burgher elements in the peasant force had gone over to them. A host of prisoners were executed in the most cruel fashion, and the rest were sent home minus their noses and ears.

---

[1] The allusion is to a popular rising in Sicily against the French Anjou dynasty which conquered Southern Italy and Sicily in 1267. In the evening of March 31, 1282, the population of Palermo massacred several thousand French knights and soldiers.—*Ed.*

Dózsa failed at Szegedin and marched on Czanád, which he captured on defeating an army of noblemen under István Báthory and Bishop Csáky. He instituted bloody reprisals for the Rákos atrocities against the prisoners, among them the Bishop and the royal Chancellor Teleki. In Czanád he proclaimed a republic, abolished the nobility, declared general equality and sovereignty of the people, and then marched against Temesvár, to which Báthory had fled. But while he besieged this fortress for two months and was reinforced by a new army under Anton Hosszú, his two army columns in Upper Hungary were defeated in several battles by the nobility. Johann Zápolya with his Transylvanian army advanced against him, attacked and dispersed the peasants. Dózsa was taken prisoner and roasted alive on a red-hot throne. His flesh was eaten by his own people, this being the condition on which their lives were spared. The dispersed peasants, reassembled by Laurentius and Hosszú, were again defeated, and those who fell into enemy hands were either impaled or hanged. The peasants' corpses hung in thousands along the roads or on the edges of gutted villages. About 60,000, it is said, either fell in battle, or were massacred. The nobility saw to it that at the next session of the Diet serfdom was again recognised as the law of the land.

The peasant revolt in the "Wendish mark", that is, Carinthia, Carniola and Styria, which broke out at about the same time, originated from a conspiracy, much like the Bundschuh. The conspirators organised and provoked an uprising as early as 1503 in that region, wrung dry by imperial officers, devastated by Turkish invasions, and tormented by famines. Already in 1513, the Slovenian and German peasants of this region once more raised the battle standard of the Stara Prawa (The Old Rights). If they allowed themselves to be placated, and if in 1514, when they gathered anew in large masses, they were again persuaded to go home by Emperor Maximilian's explicit promise to restore old rights, the war of revenge of the deceived people broke out with redoubled vigour in the spring of 1515. Just as in Hungary, castles and monasteries were destroyed everywhere, and the captured nobles were tried by peasant juries and executed. In Styria and Carinthia the

Emperor's captain, Dietrichstein, soon succeeded in crushing the revolt. In Carniola it was only suppressed by a sudden onslaught on the Rain (autumn of 1516) and the subsequent Austrian atrocities, which duplicated the infamies of the Hungarian nobility.

It is clear why, after this series of decisive defeats and the mass atrocities of the nobility, the German peasants long remained quiet. Yet conspiracies and local uprisings did not stop altogether. In 1516 most of the fugitives of the Bundschuh and the Poor Konrad returned to Swabia and the Upper Rhine, and in 1517 the Bundschuh was again in full action in the Black Forest. Joss Fritz himself, still hiding the old Bundschuh banner of 1513 on his chest, again travelled the length and breadth of the Black Forest and developed energetic activities. The conspiracy revived. Just as four years before, gatherings were held on the Kniebis. However, the secret was discovered, the authorities learned of the matter, and stepped in. Many conspirators were captured and executed. The most active and intelligent of them were compelled to flee, among them Joss Fritz, who, though he again evaded capture, seems to have died soon thereafter in Switzerland, for he is not heard of again.

IV

At the time when the fourth Bundschuh conspiracy was suppressed in the Black Forest, Luther, in Wittenberg, gave the signal for the movement that was to draw all the Estates into the vortex, and shake the whole Empire. The theses of this Augustinian[1] from Thuringia had the effect of a match held to a powder-box. The multifold and conflicting aspirations of the knights and burghers, peasants and plebeians, princes craving for sovereignty, and the lesser clergy, the clandestine mystic sects and the scholarly, satirical

---

[1] Engels refers to the 95 theses that Luther (who began his clerical career as a simple monk at the Augustinian monastery in Thuringia) nailed to a church in Wittenberg. The theses protested vigorously against the sale of indulgences and the abuses of the Catholic clergy. They also presented the initial outline of Luther's religious teaching in the vein of the cheap burgher church ideal.—*Ed.*

and burlesque[1] literary opposition, found in Luther's theses a momentarily general and common expression, and fell in with them with astounding rapidity. Formed overnight this alliance of all the dissident elements, however brief its duration, suddenly revealed the enormous power of the movement, and drove it forward very rapidly.

However, rapid growth of the movement was also bound to develop the seeds of discord that lay concealed in it. At least, it was bound to tear asunder the constituent parts of that agitated mass which, by their very place in life, were directly opposed to each other, and to return them to their normal, hostile attitude. This polarisation of the motley opposition at two centres of attraction was observed in the very first years of the Reformation. The nobility and the burghers grouped themselves unconditionally around Luther. Peasants and plebeians, as yet failing to see in Luther a direct enemy, formed, as before, a separate revolutionary party of the opposition. Yet the movement became much more general, more far-reaching, than it had been before Luther, and thereby made acute contradictions and an open conflict between the two parties inevitable. This direct antithesis soon became apparent. Luther and Münzer attacked each other in the press and pulpit, much as the armies of princes, knights and towns that for the most part consisted of Lutherans or elements at least gravitating towards Lutherism, routed the throngs of peasants and plebeians.

How strongly the interests and requirements of the various elements behind the Reformation diverged is illustrated by the attempt of the nobility to compel the princes and the clergy to meet their demands even before the Peasant War.

We have already seen the situation of the German nobility early in the sixteenth century. It was on the point of losing its independence to the ever more powerful lay and clerical princes. It saw at the same time that the decline of imperial power, the Empire breaking up into a number of

---

[1] *Burlesque*—satirical literature and parodies by writers of the Renaissance and humanitarian ideologists. They employed it to ridicule the high-flown style of court poetry and the high-handed behaviour of the upper crust of feudal society.—*Ed.*

sovereign principalities, kept pace with its own decline. It thought that its own collapse had to coincide with the collapse of the Germans as a nation. Furthermore, the nobility, and particularly that section of it which owed allegiance to the Empire, was the Estate that by virtue of its military profession and its attitude towards the princes, represented the Empire and imperial rule most distinctly. The nobility was the most national of the Estates. The stronger imperial power and German unity, and the weaker and less numerous the princes, the more powerful the nobility would become. This was the reason for the general discontent of the knighthood with Germany's pitiful political situation, with the weakness of the Empire in foreign affairs, which increased as the imperial family added to the Empire one inherited province after another, with the intrigues of foreign powers inside Germany, and with the plots by German princes and foreign countries against imperial rule. The demands of the nobility had to be, therefore, above all focused on an imperial reform, whose victims were to be the princes and the higher clergy. *Ulrich von Hutten*, the theorist of the German nobility, undertook to formulate the demand for reforms together with *Franz von Sickingen*, the nobility's military and diplomatic spokesman.

The imperial reform demanded on behalf of the nobility was conceived by Hutten in a very clear and radical manner. Hutten demanded nothing short of the elimination of all princes, secularisation of all church principalities and estates, and the establishment of *a noblemen's democracy* headed by a monarch, much like the late Polish republic in its best days. Hutten and Sickingen hoped to make the Empire united, free and powerful again through the rule of the nobility, a predominantly military class, the elimination of princes, those bearers of disunity, the annihilation of the power of the priests, and Germany's liberation from the dominance of Rome.

Founded on serfdom, this noblemen's democracy, as observed in Poland and, in somewhat modified form, in the states conquered by the Germanic tribes in the first centuries, is one of the most primitive forms of society and quite normally matures into a highly developed feudal hierarchy, a considerably higher stage. Such a pure type of noblemen's democracy was therefore impossible in 16th-century Germany. It was doubly impossible, because of the important and powerful German towns. On the other hand, alliance of the lesser nobility and the towns that in England brought about the transformation of the feudalistic into a bourgeois-constitutional monarchy, was also out of the question. In Germany the old nobility had survived, while in England it was exterminated in the Wars of the Roses down to twenty-eight families, and replaced by a new nobility of bourgeois extraction and with bourgeois tendencies; in Germany serfdom was still rampant and the nobility drew its income from *feudal* sources, while in England serfdom had been virtually abolished and the nobles had become ordinary bourgeois landowners with a *bourgeois* source of income—the ground rent. Finally, the centralisation of absolute monarchy which we see in France and which continuously developed since Louis XI in the conflict between the nobility and the burghers was impossible in Germany if only because the conditions for national centralisation were totally absent, or existed in a very rudimentary form.

Under the circumstances, the further Hutten went in putting his ideal into practice, the more concessions he was compelled to make, and the more indefinite became the outlines of his imperial reform. The nobility was not strong enough to put the reform through on its own. This was evident from its increasing weakness as compared with the princes. Allies were needed, and these could only be found in the towns, among the peasants and the influential theorists of the Reformation movement. But the towns knew the nobility too well to trust them, and rejected every offer at alliance. The peasants rightly considered the nobility, which exploited and maltreated them, as their bitterest enemy, and as to the theorists of the Reformation they held either with the burghers, the princes, or the peasants. What advantages, indeed, could the nobility promise the burghers and the peasants from an imperial reform that was mainly intended to aggrandise the nobility? Under the circumstances Hutten had no other choice but to say little or nothing in his propaganda about the future relations between the nobility, the towns and the peasants. He put all blame on the princes, the priests, and the dependence upon Rome, and showed the burghers that it was in their interests to remain at least neutral in the coming struggle between the nobility and the princes. He made no mention of abolishing serfdom or the services imposed upon the peasants by the nobility.

The attitude of the German nobility towards the peasants was at that time exactly the same as that of the Polish nobility towards its peasants in the insurrections of 1830-46. As in the modern Polish uprisings, the movement in Germany could be sustained only through an alliance of all the opposition parties, particularly the nobility and the peasants. Yet it was just this alliance that was *impossible* in both cases. The nobility did not deem it necessary to give up its political privileges and its feudal rights vis-à-vis the peasants, while the revolutionary peasants would not be drawn by vague and general prospects into an alliance with the nobility, the Estate which oppressed them most. The nobility could no more win over the peasants in Germany in 1522, than in the Poland of 1830. Only total abolition of serfdom, bondage and all privileges of the nobility could have induced the rural population to side with the nobility. But like every privileged class the nobility had not the slightest desire voluntarily to give up its privileges, its highly exclusive position, and most of its sources of income.

Thus, when the struggle finally broke out, the nobles had to face the princes alone. It came as no surprise that the princes, who had for two centuries been cutting the ground from under the nobility, gained another easy victory.

The course of the struggle is well known. In 1522 Hutten and Sickingen, who was already recognised as the political and military chief of the middle-German nobility, organised in Landau a union of the Rhenish, Swabian and Franconian nobility for a term of six years, ostensibly for self-defence. Sickingen assembled an army, partly with his own means and partly with the neighbouring knights, organised recruitment and reinforcements in Franconia, along the Lower Rhine, in the Netherlands and Westphalia, and in September 1522 opened hostilities by declaring a feud against the Elector-Archbishop of Trier. However, while he was stationed near Trier, his reinforcements were cut off by a quick intervention of the princes. The Landgrave of Hesse and the Elector Palatine came to Trier's aid and Sickingen was compelled to retreat to his castle of Landstuhl. In spite of all Hutten's efforts and those of his other friends, the united nobility, intimidated by the concerted and swift moves of the princes, left Sickingen in the lurch. Sickingen was mortally wounded, surrendered Landstuhl, and died soon afterwards. Hutten had to flee to Switzerland, where he died a few months later on the Isle of Ufnau, on the Lake of Zürich.

This defeat and the death of the two leaders broke the power of the nobility as a body independent of the princes. From then on the nobility acted only in the service and under the leadership of the princes. The Peasant War, which broke out soon after, drove the nobles to seek the direct or indirect protection of the princes. Also, it proved that the German nobility would rather continue exploiting the peasants under the dominance of the princes than overthrow the princes and priests in an open alliance with *emancipated* peasants.

V

Not a year passed since Luther's declaration of war against the Catholic hierarchy set in motion all the opposition elements in Germany without the peasants bringing forward their demands. Between 1518 and 1523 one local revolt followed another in the Black Forest and in Upper Swabia, and after the spring of 1524 revolts became systematic. In April 1524 the peasants of the Abbey of Marchthal refused to do statute labour and duties; in May the peasants of St. Blasien refused to make serf payments; in June the peasants of Steinheim, near Memmingen, announced that they would pay neither tithes nor other duties; in July and August the peasants of Thurgau revolted and were quelled partly by the mediation of Zürich and partly by the brutality of the Confederacy, which executed many of them. Finally, a more determined uprising, which may be regarded as the *direct beginning of the Peasant War*, took place in the Margraviate of Stühlingen.

The peasants of Stühlingen suddenly refused to deliver anything to the Landgrave, assembled in strong numbers, and on August 24, 1524, moved towards Waldshut under the command of *Hans Müller of Bulgenbach*. Here they founded an evangelical fraternity jointly with the burghers. The latter joined' the organisation the more willingly, because they were at odds with the government of the Austrian Forelands[1] due to the religious persecution of their preacher, Balthasar *Hubmaier*, Thomas Münzer's friend and disciple. A weekly society tax was imposed of three kreutzers—a handsome figure, considering the value of money at that time. Emissaries were sent to Alsace, the Moselle, the entire Upper Rhine and Franconia to bring peasants everywhere into the society. The society announced that its purpose was to abolish feudal rule, destroy all castles and monasteries and to eliminate all lords except the Emperor. *The German tricolour*[2] was the banner of the Union.

The uprising gained ground rapidly in all of what is now the Highland of Baden. Panic seized the nobility of Upper Swabia, whose armed forces were almost all in Italy, making war against Francis I of France. They had no choice but to drag out the affair by means of negotiations and, in the meanwhile, to collect money and recruit troops until strong enough to punish the peasants for their audacity with "burning and scorching, plundering and murdering".[3] There began that systematic betrayal, that continuous deceit and malice, which were typical of the nobility and the princes throughout the Peasant War and which were their strongest weapon against the decentralised and hard to organise peasants. The Swabian League, which consisted of the princes, the nobility and the imperial cities of Southwest Germany, put itself between the warring forces, but did

---

[1] *Austrian Forelands.* were the possessions of the Austrian Hapsburgs and their immediate vassals in Upper Swabia and the Black Forest.—*Ed.*

[2] Black-red-gold banner, which at that time and later served as the symbol of German unity.—*Ed.*

[3] Cited from the ultimatum tendered by Georg Truchsess, commander of the punitive army of the Swabian League, to the rebel peasants of Hegau on February 15, 1525, after the nobility had marshalled its counter-revolutionary forces —*Ed.*

not guarantee the peasants any real concessions. The latter remained in motion. Hans Müller of Bulgenbach marched from September 30 to the middle of October through the Black Forest to Urach and Furtwangen, increased his troops to 3,500 men and took up positions near Ewattingen (in the vicinity of Stühlingen). The nobility had no more than 1,700 men at their disposal, and even those were divided. They had to seek an armistice, which was, indeed, concluded in the camp at Ewattingen. The peasants were promised a peaceful settlement, either directly between the parties concerned or through arbitrators, and an investigation of complaints by the provincial court at Stockach. The troops of both the nobility and the peasants dispersed.

The peasants worked out sixteen clauses which they would press for in the court at Stockach. The clauses were very moderate. They went no farther than abolition of hunting rights, statute labour, oppressive taxes and privileges of lords in general, and protection against arbitrary imprisonment and biassed, arbitrary courts.

But no sooner had the peasants gone home than the nobility demanded the restoration of all controversial services pending the court decision. Naturally, the peasants refused and referred the lords to the court. The conflict flared up anew, the peasants reassembled and the princes and lords concentrated their troops. This time the movement spread farther, beyond Breisgau and into the deep of Württemberg. The troops under *Georg Truchsess* of Waldburg, the Alba of the Peasant War, watched the manoeuvres of the peasants, attacked their contingents one by one, but did not dare to attack the main force. In the meantime, Georg Truchsess negotiated with the peasant chiefs and reached agreements here and there.

By the end of December proceedings began at the Stockach provincial court. The peasants objected to the court being composed entirely of noblemen. In reply, an imperial edict[1] was read to them. The proceedings were drawn out, and in the meanwhile the nobility, the princes and the Swabian League armed themselves. Archduke

---

[1] Emperor Maximilian's edict ruled that only representatives of "noble" Estates could be members of provincial courts.—*Ed.*

Ferdinand who ruled Württemberg,[1] the Black Forest of Baden and Southern Alsace in addition to the hereditary lands which still belong to Austria, called for utmost severity against the rebel peasants. They were to be captured, tortured and mercilessly slain, wiped out in whatever way was most convenient, their possessions burned and devastated, and their wives and children driven off the land. This shows plainly how the princes and lords observed the armistice and what they meant under amicable arbitration and investigation of grievances. Archduke Ferdinand, to whom the house of Welser, of Augsburg, advanced money, armed himself in all haste. The Swabian League ordered money and a contingent of troops to be raised in three terms.

Up to this point the rebellions coincided with the five months of Thomas Münzer's presence in the Highland. There is no direct proof of his involvement in the outbreak and course of the movement, but, indirectly, it has been fully ascertained. The more resolute of the peasant revolutionaries were mostly his disciples, and put forward his ideas. The Twelve Articles and the Letter of Articles of the Highland peasants are ascribed to him by all his contemporaries, although, beyond any doubt, he had no part in composing at least the former. When still on his way back to Thuringia, he addressed a bold revolutionary manifesto to the insurgent peasants.[2]

Duke Ulrich, exiled from Württemberg in 1519, conspired to regain his land with the aid of the peasants. Ever since he was exiled he had been trying to utilise the revolutionary party, and had supported it continuously. His name was associated with most of the local disturbances between

---

[1] After Duke Ulrich was banished in 1519 by the Swabian League and the dissentient Württemberg nobility and burghers, Württemberg passed under the rule of the Austrian Archduke.—*Ed.*

[2] Engels refers to the anonymous pamphlet printed in Nuremberg in early 1525, entitled *To the Assembly of All the Indignant and Insurgent Peasantry of the Upper German Nation and Many Other Places on Whether or Not Its Indignation Is Just and What It Should or Should Not Do to the Authorities. Based on the Holy Scripture, Composed and Rendered With the Full Approval of the Highland Brotherhood.* (See W. Zimmermann, *Allgemeine Geschichte des grossen Bauernkrieges*, T. 2, Stuttgart, 1842, S. 113-15.)—*Ed.*

1520 and 1524 in the Black Forest and in Württemberg. Now he was arming for an attack on Württemberg from his castle, Hohentwiel. However, he too was only being

Title page of the *Letter of Articles* spread by the revolutionary peasants

used by the peasants, had no influence over them, and very little of their trust.

The winter passed, but nothing decisive was undertaken by either side. The princely masters went into hiding. The peasant revolt was gaining in scale. In January 1525 the entire country between the Danube, the Rhine and the

Lech was in a ferment, and in February the storm broke loose.

While the *Black Forest and Hegau Troop* under Hans Müller of Bulgenbach was conspiring with Ulrich of Württemberg and shared part of his futile march on Stuttgart (February and March 1525), the peasants in Ried, above the Ulm, rose on February 9, assembled in a camp near Baltringen protected on all sides by marshes, hoisted the *red flag*, and formed the *Baltringen Troop* under the leadership of Ulrich Schmidt. This troop was 10,000 to 12,000 strong.

On February 25, the 7,000-strong *Upper Allgäu Troop* assembled at Schussen, impelled by the rumour that troops were marching against the discontented elements who had appeared in this locality as everywhere else. The people of Kempten, who had been at odds with their archbishop all winter, assembled the next day and joined the peasants. The towns of Memmingen and Kaufbeuren joined the movement after laying down their conditions; yet the ambiguous attitude of the towns in this struggle was already apparent. On March 7 twelve articles were adopted in Memmingen for all the peasants of Upper Allgäu.

Tidings from the Allgäu peasants prompted the formation of a *Lake Troop* under Eitel Hans on Lake Constance. It grew very quickly and established its headquarters in Bermatingen.

Similarly, early in March the peasants arose in Lower Allgäu, in the region of Ochsenhausen and Schellenberg, in Zeil and Waldburg, the estates of Truchsess. This *Lower Allgäu Troop*, which consisted of 7,000 men, had its camp near Wurzach.

These four troops accepted all the Memmingen articles, more moderate even than the Hegau articles, because they showed a remarkable lack of determination in points relating to the attitude of the armed troops towards the nobility and the government. Such determination as was shown appeared only in the course of the war, after the peasants experienced the mode of action of their enemies.

At the same time, a sixth troop formed on the Danube. Peasants from the entire region, from Ulm to Donauwörth, from the valleys of the Iller, Roth and Biber, came to Leipheim and made camp there. Every able-bodied man from fifteen localities had come there, while reinforcements were drawn from 117. The leader of the *Leipheim Troop* was Ulrich Schön, and its preacher was [Hans] Jakob Wehe, the pastor of Leipheim.

Thus, in the beginning of March there were 30,000 to 40,000 insurgent Upper Swabian peasants under arms in six camps. The peasant troops were a mixed lot. Münzer's revolutionary party was in the minority everywhere. Yet it formed the backbone of all the peasant camps. The bulk of the peasants were always ready to come to terms with the lords wherever they were promised the concessions they hoped to gain by their menacing attitude. As the uprising dragged on and the princes' armies drew nearer, they grew war-weary and most of those who still had something to lose, went home. Moreover, vagabond masses of the lumpenproletariat had joined the troops and this undermined their discipline and demoralised the peasants, because the vagabonds came and went as they pleased. This alone is enough to explain why the peasants at first remained everywhere on the defensive, why their morale deteriorated in the camps and why, aside from their tactical shortcomings and the shortage of good leaders, they were no match for the armies of the princes.

While the troops were still assembling, Duke Ulrich invaded Württemberg from Hohentwiel with recruited detachments and a few Hegau peasants. The Swabian League would have been lost if the peasants had used the opportunity to attack the troops of Truchsess von Waldburg from the other flank. But because of the defensive attitude of the peasantry, Truchsess soon succeeded in concluding an armistice with the Baltringen, Allgäu and Lake peasants, in starting negotiations, and fixing Judica Sunday (April 2)[1] as the day on which the whole affair was to be settled. This gave him a chance to march against Duke Ulrich, to occupy Stuttgart, and to compel him to abandon Württemberg again on March 17. Then he turned against the peasants, but the lansquenets in his own army revolted and refused to march. Truchsess succeeded in placating

---

[1] *Judica Sunday*—the fifth Sunday in Lent.—*Ed.*

the mutineers and moved towards Ulm, where new reinforcements were being formed. He left an observation post at Kirchheim near Teck.

The Swabian League, which at last had its hands free and had gathered its first contingents, threw off its mask, declaring itself "determined to end with arms in hand and with the aid of God that which the peasants have wilfully undertaken".[1]

The peasants had meanwhile observed the armistice in all strictness. They had drawn up their demands, the famous *Twelve Articles*, for the negotiations on Judica Sunday. They demanded the right to elect and depose clergymen through the communities; abolition of the small tithe and utilisation of the great tithe[2], after subtraction of the pastors' salaries, for public purposes; abolition of serfdom and of death tolls; the right to fish and hunt; restriction of excessive statute labour, taxes and ground rents; restitution of forests, pastures and privileges forcibly withdrawn from communities and individuals, and elimination of arbitrary justice and administration. Clearly, the moderate, conciliatory element still had the upper hand among the peasant troops. The revolutionary party had formulated its programme earlier in the *Letter of Articles*. It was an open letter to all the peasants, calling on them to join "the Christian Alliance and Brotherhood" for the purpose of removing all burdens either through goodwill, "which was unlikely" or by force, and threatening all shirkers with "lay anathema", i.e., with expulsion from the communities and from all intercourse with members of the Brotherhood. All castles, monasteries and priests' endowments were also

---

[1] This decision was made at a conference of League authorities at Ulm in March 1525, at a time when representatives of the Swabian League were still conducting negotiations with the insurgents. It is recorded in a document from the Ulm archive and quoted by Zimmermann (see W. Zimmermann, *Allgemeine Geschichte des grossen Bauernkrieges,* T. 2, Stuttgart, 1842, S. 167).

[2] *Small* and *great tithe*—two varieties of a highly oppressive duty paid by peasants in favour of the Catholic Church. The size and nature of this tax varied in different parts of Germany, and in most cases greatly exceeded a tenth of the peasants' produce. As a rule, the small tithe was imposed on cattle, while the great tithe applied to the harvest.—*Ed.*

to be placed under lay anathema, the letter said, unless the nobility, the priests and monks relinquished them of their own accord, moved into ordinary houses like other people, and joined the Christian Alliance. This radical manifesto, obviously composed *before* the spring insurrection of 1525, thus speaks above all of revolution, of complete victory

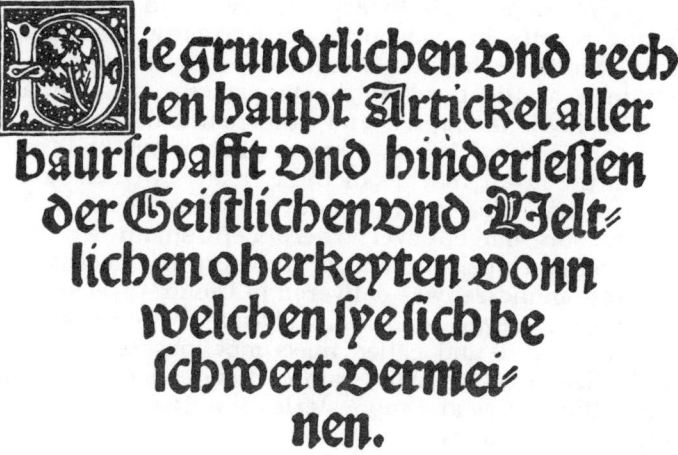

Headline to the Twelve Articles outlining the peasants' demands

over the classes still in rule, while the "lay anathema" is designed for oppressors and traitors who were to be killed, for the castles that were to be burned, and the monasteries and endowments that were to be confiscated and whose treasures were to be turned into cash.

But before the peasants came to present their Twelve Articles to the proper courts of arbitration, they learned that the Swabian League had violated the armistice and that its troops were approaching. Instantly, they took countermeasures. A general meeting of all Allgäu, Baltringen and Lake peasants was held at Geisbeuren. The four troops were combined and reorganised into four columns. A decision was made to confiscate the church estates, to sell their treasures in favour of the war chest, and to burn the castles. Thus, alongside the official Twelve Articles, the

Letter of Articles became the statute of warfare, and Judica Sunday, the day designated for the conclusion of peace, became the date of a *general uprising*.

The mounting unrest everywhere, continuous local conflicts between peasants and nobility, tidings of the uprising in the Black Forest, which had been brewing in the preceding six months, and of its spread to the Danube and the Lech, are enough to explain the rapid succession of peasant revolts in two-thirds of Germany. But that the single revolts broke out simultaneously proves that there were men at the head of the movement who organised them through Anabaptist and other emissaries. Already in the second half of March disorders broke out in Württemberg, in the lower reaches of the Neckar, in Odenwald, and in Lower and Middle Franconia. However, April 2, Judica Sunday, was named everywhere beforehand as the day of the general uprising, and everywhere the decisive blow, the revolt en masse, was delivered in the first week of April. The Allgäu, Hegau and Lake peasants also sounded the bells on April 1 and called mass meetings to summon all able-bodied men to their camp; they opened hostilities against the castles and monasteries simultaneously with the Baltringen peasants.

In *Franconia*, where the movement had six centres, the insurrection broke out everywhere in the first days of April. At about the same time two peasant camps were formed near *Nördlingen*, with whose aid the revolutionary party of the town under *Anton Forner* gained the upper hand, appointed Forner town mayor, and consummated a union between the town and the peasants. In the region of *Ansbach* the peasants revolted everywhere between April 1 and 7, and from here the uprising spread to Bavaria. In the region of *Rothenburg* the peasants were under arms since March 22. In the town of Rothenburg the rule of the honourables was overthrown by the petty burghers and the plebeians under Stephan von *Menzingen*, but since peasant dues were the chief source of revenue for the town, the new government also vacillated and acted ambiguously towards the peasants. A general uprising of peasants and townships broke out early in April in the Grand Chapter of *Würzburg,* and in the bishopric of *Bamberg* a general insurrection compelled the bishop to yield within five days. A strong *Bildhausen peasant camp* formed in the North, on the border of Thuringia.

In *Odenwald*, where *Wendel Hipler*, nobleman and former chancellor of the Counts von Hohenlohe, and *Georg Metzler*, an innkeeper from Ballenberg near Krautheim, headed the revolutionary party, the storm broke out on March 26. The peasants marched from all directions towards the Tauber. The two thousand men of the Rothenburg camp joined them. Georg Metzler took command and upon the arrival of all his reinforcements marched on April 4 to the monastery of Schönthal on the Jagst, where he was joined by the peasants of the *Neckar valley*. The latter, led by *Jäcklein Rohrbach*, an innkeeper from Böckingen near Heilbronn, had begun their insurrection in Flein, Sontheim, etc., on Judica Sunday, while Wendel Hipler took Öhringen by surprise with a number of conspirators and drew the peasants in the vicinity into the movement. In Schönthal the two peasant columns combined into the *Gay Troop*, accepted the Twelve Articles and made a few raids on castles and monasteries. The Gay Troop was about 8,000 strong and had cannon and 3,000 muskets. *Florian Geyer*, a Franconian knight, joined the force and formed the Black Troop, a select corps recruited mainly from the Rothenburg and Öhringen Landwehr.

The Württemberg magistrate in Neckarsulm, Count Ludwig von Helfenstein, opened the hostilities. He ordered all captured peasants to be executed on the spot. The Gay Troop marched to meet him. The peasants were embittered by the massacres and by news of the defeat of the Leipheim Troop, of Hans Jakob Wehe's execution, and the Truchsess atrocities. Von Helfenstein, who had moved into Weinsberg, was there attacked. The castle was stormed by Florian Geyer, the town seized in a prolonged battle and Count Ludwig taken prisoner along with several knights. On the following day, April 17, Jäcklein Rohrback and the most resolute members of the troop held court over the prisoners and made fourteen of them, with von Helfenstein at their head, run the gauntlet, this being the most humiliating death they could think of. The capture of Weinsberg and Jäcklein's terroristic revenge on von Helfenstein did not fail to have their effect on the nobility. The Counts von Löwenstein joined the peasant alliance. The Counts von Hohenlohe, who had joined previously but had given no aid, immediately sent the desired cannons and powder.

The chiefs debated among themselves whether they should make Götz von Berlichingen their commander, "since he could bring to them the nobility". The proposal found sympathy, but Florian Geyer, who saw the seeds of reaction in this mood of the peasants and their chiefs, separated from the Gay Troop and marched on his own with his Black Troop, first through the Neckar and then the Würzburg region, everywhere destroying castles and lairs of priests.

The rest of the troops marched against Heilbronn. In this powerful free imperial town the patriciate was, as almost everywhere, confronted by a burgher and revolutionary opposition. In secret agreement with the peasants, the latter opened the gates to Georg Metzler and Jäcklein Rohrbach on April 17 during a disturbance. The peasant chiefs and their people took possession of the town, which was then admitted to their brotherhood and delivered 1,200 guilders in cash and a squad of volunteers. Only the possessions of the clergy and the Teutonic Order[1] were pillaged. On April 22, the peasants moved out, leaving a small garrison. Heilbronn was to become the centre of the various troops, the latter actually sending delegates and conferring over joint actions and the common demands of the peasantry. But the burgher opposition and the patricians, who had joined forces after the peasant invasion, regained the upper hand in the town, preventing decisive

---

[1] *Teutonic Order*—a German religious order of knights founded in 1190 during the crusades. The Order seized numerous possessions in Germany and other countries. These were administered by commandores. In the 13th century, East Prussia fell under the rule of the Order after it was overrun and the local Lithuanian population was exterminated. This possession became a seat of aggression against Poland, Lithuania and the adjoining Russian principalities. In 1237 the Order amalgamated with the Livonian Order, which also had its seat in the Baltic area. After the defeat at Chudskoye Lake in 1242 and in the Grünwald Battle in 1410, the Order declined rapidly and was able to maintain only a small part of its former possessions.—*Ed.*

steps and waiting only for the approach of the princes' troops to betray the peasants.

The peasants marched toward Odenwald. Götz von Berlichingen, who had a few days before offered himself to the Grand Elector Palatine, then to the peasantry, and then again to the Elector, was to join the Evangelist Fraternity on April 24 and assume supreme command of the Gay *Bright* Troop (as distinct from the *Black* Troop of Florian Geyer). At the same time, however, he was the prisoner of the peasants, who mistrusted him and bound him to a council of chiefs, without whose approval he could undertake nothing. Götz and Metzler marched with the bulk of the peasants across Buchen to Amorbach, where, during their stay from April 30 to May 5, they roused the entire Main region. The nobility was everywhere compelled to join in, and its castles were thus spared. Only the monasteries were burned and pillaged. The troop had become visibly demoralised. The most energetic men had gone away with Florian Geyer or with Jäcklein Rohrbach who, after the capture of Heilbronn, also separated from the troop, apparently because he, the judge of Count von Helfenstein, could no longer remain with a body that was inclined towards reconciliation with the nobility. This inclination towards an understanding with the nobility was in itself a sign of demoralisation. Soon Wendel Hipler proposed a very sound reorganisation of the troop. He suggested that the lansquenets, who had been offering their services daily, should be taken on. He also suggested that the troop should no longer be renewed monthly through the arrival of fresh contingents and the dismissal of old ones, and that the men under arms, who had received a certain amount of military training, should be retained. But the general assembly rejected both proposals. The peasants had become blustery and viewed the war as little more than pillage in which the competition of the lansquenets held no advantage for them; they wanted to be free to go home as soon as their pockets were full. In Amorbach matters came to a point where Hans Berlin, a Heilbronn councillor, induced the chiefs and troop councils to accept a "Declaration of the Twelve Articles", a document wherein the remaining edges of the Twelve Articles were blunted and words of humble supplication were put into the mouths of the peasants. But this was too much for the peasants; they rejected the Declaration with a display of vehemence and insisted upon the original Articles.

In the meantime, a decisive change had taken place in the Würzburg area. The bishop who had withdrawn to fortified Frauenberg near Würzburg after the first uprising early in April and had vainly sent messages in all directions asking for aid, was finally compelled to make temporary concessions. On May 2 a Diet opened in which the peasants were represented, but letters proving the bishop's treacherous moves were intercepted before any results could be achieved. The Diet broke up at once, and hostilities began between the insurgent townsmen and peasants, on the one hand, and the bishop's forces, on the other. The bishop escaped to Heidelberg on May 5, and on the following day Florian Geyer with his Black Troop entered Würzburg, and with him came the *Franconian Tauber Troop*, which consisted of the peasants of Mergentheim, Rothenburg and Ansbach. On May 7 Götz von Berlichingen arrived with his Cay Bright Troop and the siege of Frauenberg began.

In Limburg and the Ellwangen and Hall regions another contingent was formed by the end of March, and in early April that of *Gaildorf*, or the *Common Gay Troop*. It showed considerable violence, roused the entire region, burned down many monasteries and castles, including the castle of Hohenstaufen, compelled all the peasants to join it, and made the nobles, and even the cup-bearers of Limburg, to enter the Christian Alliance. Early in May it invaded Württemberg, but was compelled to withdraw. The separatism of the German system of small states, as in 1848, obstructed joint action by the revolutionaries of the various states. The Gaildorf Troop, restricted to a small area, was naturally bound to disperse when all resistance within that area was broken. It concluded an agreement with the town of Gmünd, and went home, leaving only 500 under arms.

In the *Palatinate* peasant troops were formed on either bank of the Rhine by the end of April. They destroyed many castles and monasteries, and on May 1 took Neustadt on the Hardt after the Bruchrain peasants had crossed the river on the previous day and forced Speyer to conclude an agreement. The Marshal of Habern at the head of the Elector's small force was powerless against them, and on May 10 the Elector was compelled to come to an agreement with the peasants, guaranteeing them redress through the Diet.

Finally, in *Württemberg* the revolt broke out early in separate localities. The peasants of the Urach Alp formed a union against the priests and lords as early as February and the peasants of Blaubeuren, Urach, Münsingen, Balingen and Rosenfeld revolted late in March. The Württemberg region was invaded by the Gaildorf Troop at Göppingen, by Jäcklein Rohrbach at Brackenheim and by the remnants of the beaten Leipheim Troop at Pfullingen, inciting the rural population to revolt. There were also serious disturbances in other localities. On April 6 Pfullingen surrendered to the peasants. The Austrian Archduke's government was driven to the wall. It had no money and only few troops. The cities and castles were in bad condition and had neither garrisons nor munition. Even Asperg was practically defenseless.

The government's attempt to call out town reserves against the peasants caused its instant defeat. On April 16 the Bottwar town reserves refused to obey orders. Instead of marching to Stuttgart, they turned to Wunnenstein near Bottwar, where they formed the nucleus of a camp of burghers and peasants whose number multiplied rapidly. The rebellion in Zabergau broke out on the same day. The Maulbronn monastery was pillaged and a number of monasteries and castles was razed to the ground. The Gäu peasants received reinforcements from neighbouring Bruchrain.

The Wunnenstein troop was under the command of *Matern Feuerbacher*, a Bottwar town councillor. He was a leader of the burgher opposition, but sufficiently compromised to be compelled to join the peasants. However, he remained at all times very moderate, prevented application of the Letter of Articles to the castles, and sought everywhere to reconcile the peasants with the moderate burgherdom. He prevented the amalgamation of the Württemberg peasants with the Gay Bright Troop, and later also prevailed on the Gaildorf Troop to withdraw from Württemberg. On April 19 he was deposed for his burgher tendencies, but was again made commander the next day. He was indispensable, and even when Jäcklein Rohrbach arrived with 200 of his associates to join the Württemberg peasants on April 22, he had no choice but to leave Feuerbacher in command, and confined himself to rigid supervision of his actions.

On April 18 the government attempted to negotiate with the peasants stationed at Wunnenstein. The peasants insisted upon the Twelve Articles, but the government representatives naturally rejected them. The troop set itself into motion. On April 20 it reached Laufen, where, for the last time, it turned down the proposals of the government delegates. On April 22 the troop, numbering 6,000, appeared in Bietigheim and threatened Stuttgart. Most of the Town Council had fled and a citizens' committee took over the administration. Among the citizenry there was, as elsewhere, the same division into parties of the honourables, the burgher opposition, and the revolutionary plebeians. On April 25 the latter opened the gates to the peasants and Stuttgart was instantly taken. The formation of the *Gay Christian Troop,* as the Württemberg insurgents now called themselves, was here consummated and rigid rules were established for pay, division of booty, maintenance, etc. A detachment of Stuttgarters, under Theus Gerber, joined the troop.

On April 29 Feuerbacher marched with all his men against the Gaildorfers, who had entered the Württemberg region at Schorndorf. He drew the entire region into his alliance and thus persuaded the Gaildorfers to withdraw. In this way he prevented the revolutionary element in his troop under Rohrbach from fusing with the reckless Gaildorf troop and thus obtaining dangerous reinforcements. Upon receiving news of Truchsess' approach, he left Schorndorf to meet him, and on May 1 made camp near Kirchheim-unter-Teck.

We have thus traced the origin and development of the uprising in that portion of Germany which we must regard as the territory of the first group of peasant armies. Before we proceed to the other groups (Thuringia and Hesse, Alsace, Austria and the Alps) we must give an account of

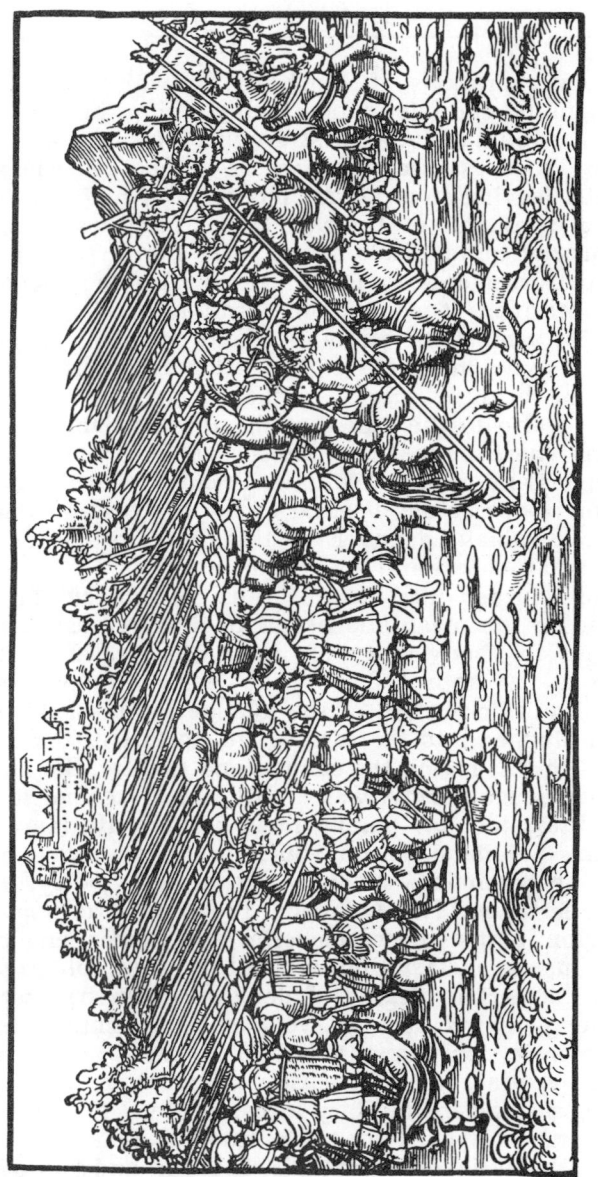

Peasant troops on the march

the military operations of Truchsess, in which he, alone at the beginning and later supported by various princes and townships, annihilated this first group of insurgents.

We left Truchsess near Ulm, where he had come late in March after leaving an observation corps in Kirchheim Teck under the command of Dietrich Spät. Truchsess' corps, which was not quite 10,000 strong after the arrival of the League reinforcements, concentrated in Ulm and included 7,200 infantrymen; it was the only army at his disposal for an offensive against the peasants. Reinforcements came to Ulm very slowly, due partly to the difficulties of recruiting in insurgent localities, partly to the government's lack of money, and also to the fact that the few available troops were everywhere more than indispensable for manning the fortresses and castles. We have already oted the small number of troops at the disposal of the princes and towns outside the Swabian League. Everything therefore depended upon Georg Truchsess and his League army.

Truchsess turned first against the *Baltringen Troop*, which had in the meantime begun to destroy castles and monasteries in the vicinity of Ried. The peasants, who withdrew at the approach of the League troops, were outflanked and driven out of the marshes, crossed the Danube and plunged into the ravines and forests of the Swabian Alps. In this region the cannon and cavalry, the mainstay of the League army, was of little avail against them, and Truchsess did not pursue them farther. He marched against the Leipheim Troop which numbered 5,000 men stationed at Leipheim, 4,000 in the Mindel valley, and 6,000 at Illertissen. The Leipheim Troop was rousing the entire region, destroying monasteries and castles, and preparing to march against Ulm with all its three columns. It seems that a certain degree of demoralisation had set in among the peasants here as well, and undermined their military morale, for [Hans] Jakob Wehe tried at the very outset to negotiate with Truchsess. The latter, however, backed by a sufficient military force, declined to negotiate and on April 4 attacked the main troop at Leipheim, and routed it. [Hans] Jakob Wehe, Ulrich Schön and two other peasant leaders were captured and beheaded; Leipheim capitulated, and several expeditions to the adjacent countryside subdued the entire region.

A new rebellion of the lansquenets, who demanded plunder and additional pay, delayed Truchsess again until April 10, when he marched southwest against the *Baltringen Troop* which had, in the meantime, invaded his estates, Waldburg, Zeil and Wolfegg, and besieged his castles. Here, also, he found the peasants disunited, and defeated them on April 11 and 12 successively in isolated battles, which completely disrupted the Baltringen Troop. Its remnants withdrew under the command of priest Florian and joined the *Lake Troop*. Truchsess now turned against the latter. The Lake Troop, which had meanwhile more than merely roved through the countryside, and had also drawn the towns of Buchhorn (Friedrichshafen) and Wollmatingen into the fraternity, held a big military council in the monastery of Salem on April 13 and decided to move against Truchsess. Alarm bells were sounded at once, and 10,000 men, joined by the defeated Baltringen Troop, assembled in the Bermatingen camp. On April 15 they stood their ground in a battle with Truchsess, who did not want to risk his army in a decisive battle and preferred to negotiate, strengthened in this purpose by news of the approach of the Allgäu and Hegau troops. On April 17 he therefore concluded an agreement with the Lake and Baltringen peasants in Weingarten. On the face of it, the agreement was quite favourable for them, and they accepted it without hesitation. Ultimately, he also induced delegates of the Upper and Lower Allgäu peasants to accept this agreement, and marched towards Württemberg.

Truchsess' cunning saved him from certain defeat. Had he not succeeded in fooling the weak, dull-witted, for the most part already demoralised peasants and their mostly incapable, timid and venal leaders, he and his small army would have been enveloped by four columns of at least 25,000 to 30,000 men, and would inevitably have lost. It was his enemies' narrow-mindedness, always unavoidable among peasants, that enabled him to get rid of them at the very moment when they could have ended the war with one blow, at least as far as Swabia and Franconia were concerned. The Lake peasants observed the agreement, which was naturally turned against them in the long run, so rigidly that they later took up arms against their allies, the Hegau peasants. Although the Allgäu peasants, involved in the betrayal by their leaders, soon renounced the agreement, Truchsess was by then out of danger.

The Hegau peasants, though they were not bound by the Weingarten agreement, soon gave a new display of the infinite narrow-mindedness and stubborn provincialism that proved the undoing of the entire Peasant War. When, after futile negotiations with them, Truchsess marched off to Württemberg, they followed him and were continually on his flank; but it did not occur to them to unite with the Württemberg Gay Christian Troop, and this because previously the peasants of Württemberg and the Neckar valley had refused them assistance. When Truchsess had marched far enough from their home country, they turned back placidly and marched on Freiburg.

We left the Württemberg peasants under the command of Matern Feuerbacher at Kirchheim-unter-Teck, from where the observation corps left by Truchsess under the command of Dietrich Spät had withdrawn towards Urach. After an unsuccessful attempt to take Urach, Feuerbacher turned towards Nürtingen and sent messages to all insurgent troops in the vicinity to assist him in the decisive battle. Considerable reinforcements came from both the Württemberg lowlands and from Gäu. The Gäu peasants, who had joined the remnants of the Leipheim Troop that had withdrawn to West Württemberg and roused the entire valleys of the Upper Neckar and Nagold up to Böblingen and Leonberg, came in two strong columns to join Feuerbacher at Nürtingen on May 5. Truchsess ran into the united troop at Böblingen. Its number, its artillery and position perplexed him. In his usual manner, he at once started to negotiate and concluded an armistice with the peasants. But no sooner had he thus secured his position than he attacked them on May 12 *during the armistice* and forced a decisive battle on them. The peasants offered long and courageous resistance until Böblingen finally surrendered to Truchsess owing to the betrayal of the burghers. The left wing of the peasants, deprived of its base of support, was forced back and outflanked. This decided the issue. The undisciplined peasants were thrown into confusion, and thereupon took to disorderly flight; those of them who were not killed or captured by League horsemen threw away their weapons and hurried home. The Gay Christian Troop, and with it the whole Württemberg insurrection, were crushed. Theus Gerber fled to Esslingen and Feuerbacher to Switzerland, while Jäcklein Rohrbach was taken prisoner and dragged in chains to Neckargartach, where he was chained to a stake, surrounded by firewood and roasted to death on a slow fire, while Truchsess, carousing with his knights, gloated over this knightly spectacle.

From Neckargartach Truchsess supported the operations of the Elector Palatine by invading Kraichgau. On receiving word of Truchsess' success, the Elector, who meanwhile had gathered troops, immediately broke his agreement with the peasants, attacked Bruchrain on May 23, captured and burned Malsch after a vigorous resistance, pillaged a number of villages, and garrisoned Bruchsal. At the same time Truchsess attacked Eppingen and captured the chief of the local movement, Anton Eisenhut, whom the Elector immediately executed with nearly a dozen other peasant leaders. Bruchrain and Kraichgau were thus subdued and compelled to pay an indemnity of about 40,000 guilders. Both armies, that of Truchsess—reduced to 6,000 men in the preceding battles—and that of the Elector (6,500 men), united and moved against the Odenwalders.

Word of the Böblingen defeat spread terror everywhere among the insurgents. The free imperial cities which had come under the heavy hand of the peasants, heaved a sigh of relief. The city of Heilbronn was the first to seek reconciliation with the Swabian League. In Heilbronn the peasants' office and delegates of the various troops deliberated over the proposals they would make to the Emperor and the Empire in the name of all the insurgent peasants. These negotiations, whose outcome was to apply to all Germany, revealed again that none of the existing Estates, including the peasants, was sufficiently developed to reshape the situation in Germany according to its own viewpoint. It was obvious at once that the support of the nobility and particularly of the burghers had to be gained for this purpose. *Wendel Hipier* took charge of the negotiations. Of all the leaders of the movement he had the best grasp on the existing situation. He was not a far-seeing revolutionary like Münzer, not a peasant representative like Metzler or Rohrbach; his extensive experience and his practical knowledge of the attitude of the various Estates towards each other prevented him from representing any one of the Estates involved in the movement in opposition to the others. Just as Münzer, a representative of the budding proletariat, which then stood outside the existing official organisation of society, was driven to anticipate communism, Wendel Hipler, the representative, as it were, of the cross-section of the nation's progressive elements, anticipated *modern bourgeois society*. The principles he represented and the demands he made were not really immediately practicable. They were the somewhat idealised, and inevitable, result of the dissolution of feudal society. And the peasants, having set themselves to drafting legislation for the whole Empire, were compelled to accept them. The centralisation thus demanded by the peasants assumed in Heilbronn a definite form, which was, however, worlds removed from the peasants' own idea of it. It was, for instance, much more clearly defined in the demands for standard currency, weights and measures, and the abolition of internal customs, etc., that is, in demands which were far more in the interests of townsmen than in those of the peasants. Concessions were made to the nobility which substantially approached the modern system of redemption, and would in the long run transform feudal landownership into bourgeois ownership. In a word, since the peasant demands were framed as a system of "imperial reform", they did not embody the immediate demands of the peasantry, but became necessarily subordinate to definite burgher interests.

While this imperial reform was still being debated in Heilbronn, the author of the "Declaration of the Twelve Articles", Hans Berlin, was already on his way to meet Truchsess and negotiate the surrender of the township on behalf of the honourables and burghers. Reactionary movements within the town supported this betrayal, and Wendel Hipler was obliged to flee with the peasants. He went to Weinsberg where he attempted to assemble the remnants of the Württemberg Troop and the scanty mobile unit of Gaildorfers. But the approach of the Elector Palatine and Truchsess drove him from there as well, and he was compelled to go to Würzburg to rouse the Gay Bright Troop into action. In the meantime, the armies of the League and the Elector subdued the entire Neckar region, compelled the peasants to renew their oath of allegiance, burned many villages, and beheaded or hanged all escaped peasants that fell into their hands. Weinsberg was burned to avenge the execution of von Helfenstein.

The peasants assembled near Würzburg had in the meantime laid siege to Frauenberg, and on May 15, before even a breach was made in the wall of the fortress, they bravely but unsuccessfully attempted to storm it. Four hundred of the best men, mostly of Florian Geyer's Troop, were left behind in the ditches, dead or wounded. Two days later, on May 17, Wendel Hipler arrived and ordered a military council. He proposed to leave only 4,000 men at Frauenberg, and to encamp with the main force of about 20,000 men at Krautheim on the Jagst under the very nose of Truchsess, so that all reinforcements might be concentrated there. It was an excellent plan. Only by keeping the masses together, and by numerical superiority, could the peasants hope to defeat the princely army, which now numbered about 13,000 men. The demoralisation and discouragement of the peasants, however, was too far gone to contemplate any energetic action. Götz von Berlichingen, who soon turned traitor, may also have helped to hold the Troop back, and Hipler's plan was thus never executed. Instead, the forces were split up as usual, and only on May 23 did the Gay Bright Troop go into action after the Franconians promised to follow without delay. On May 26 the Ansbach detachments encamped in Würzburg were induced to return home on receiving word that their Margrave[1] had opened hostilities against the peasants. The rest of the besieging army, along with Florian Geyer's Black Troop, occupied positions at Heidingsfeld in the vicinity of Würzburg.

---

[1] Allusion is made to Casimir, Margrave of Brandenburg, who was in possession of Ansbach and Beireit.—*Ed.*

On May 24 the Gay Bright Troop arrived in Krautheim none too ready for battle. Many learned here that in their absence their villages had sworn allegiance to Truchsess, and used this as a pretext to go home. The troop moved on to Neckarsulm, and on May 28 started negotiations with Truchsess. At the same time messengers were sent to the peasants of Franconia, Alsace and Black Forest-Hegau to ask for rapid reinforcements. From Neckarsulm Götz [von Berlichingen] marched back to Öhringen. The troop melted away day after day. Götz von Berlichingen also disappeared during the march. He had gone home, having previously negotiated with Truchsess through his old brother-in-arms, Dietrich Spät, about going over to the other side. In Öhringen a false rumour of the enemy's approach threw the perplexed and discouraged peasantry into a panic. The troop ran off in all directions, and it was with difficulty that Metzler and Wendel Hipler succeeded in keeping together about 2,000 men, whom they again led toward Krautheim. In the meantime, the Franconian army of 5,000 men had come, but due to a side march through Löwenstein towards Öhringen, ordered by Götz with obviously treacherous intentions, it missed the Gay Troop and moved towards Neckarsulm. This town, defended by several detachments of the Gay Bright Troop, was besieged by Truchsess. The Franconians arrived at night and saw the fires of the League army, but their leaders had not the courage to venture an attack and retreated to Krautheim where they at last found the remainder of the Gay Bright Troop. Receiving no aid, Neckarsulm surrendered to the League force on May 29. At once Truchsess had thirteen peasants executed, and marched against the troop, burning and ravaging, pillaging and murdering on the way. His route through the valleys of the Neckar, Kocher and Jagst was marked with ruins and the corpses of peasants hanging on trees.

At Krautheim the League army overtook the peasants. Truchsess outflanked them and forced them to withdraw towards Königshofen-on-the-Tauber. Here they took up their position, 8,000 strong and with 32 cannons. Truchsess approached them behind the cover of hills and forests. He sent out columns to envelop them, and on June 2 attacked them with such greatly superior forces and with so much energy that they were defeated and dispersed in spite of the stubborn resistance of several columns that lasted into the night. As everywhere, it was the League horsemen, the "Peasants' Death", who were mainly instrumental in annihilating the insurgent army, charging down upon the peasants shaken by artillery and musket fire and lance attacks, breaking their ranks completely and slaying them one by one. The kind of warfare Truchsess and his horsemen led is illustrated by the fate of 300 Königshofen burghers who had joined the peasant army. All but fifteen of them were killed in the battle and four were subsequently beheaded.

Having thus settled with the peasants of Odenwald, the Neckar valley and Lower Franconia, Truchsess subdued the whole region in a series of punitive expeditions, burning down villages and executing countless people. Then he marched against Würzburg. On the way he learned that the second Franconian Troop under Florian Geyer and Gregor von Burgbernheim was stationed at Sulzdorf, and instantly turned against it.

After his unsuccessful storming of Frauenberg, Florian Geyer had mainly devoted himself to negotiating with the princes and towns, especially with Rothenburg and Margrave Casimir of Ansbach, urging them to join the peasant fraternity, but was suddenly recalled by the news of the Königshofen defeat. His troop was joined by that of Ansbach under Gregor von Burgbernheim. The Ansbach troop was only recently formed. Margrave Casimir had managed to keep in check the peasant revolt in his possessions in true Hohenzollern style, partly with promises and partly with the threat of massed troops. He maintained complete neutrality towards all outside troops as long as they did not recruit Ansbach subjects, and tried to direct the hatred of the peasants mainly against the church endowments, through whose ultimate confiscation he hoped to enrich himself. In the meantime, he kept arming, and biding his time. As soon as he learned of the Böblingen battle he opened hostilities against his rebellious peasants, pillaging and burning their villages and hanging or otherwise killing many of them. But the peasants rallied quickly and defeated him at Windsheim under the command of Gregor von Burgbernheim on May 29. The call of the hard-pressed Odenwald peasants reached them as they were still pursuing him, and they headed at once for Heidingsfeld and from there, with Florian Geyer, again towards Würzburg (June 2). Still without word from the Odenwald troop, they left behind 5,000 peasants in Würzburg and with 4,000—the rest having deserted—they followed the others. Made complacent by false news of the outcome of the Königshofen battle, they were attacked by Truchsess at *Sulzdorf* and completely defeated. Truchsess' horsemen and lansquenets staged the usual massacre. Florian Geyer rallied the remainder of his Black Troop, 600 in number, and fought his way to the village of Ingoldstadt. Two hundred occupied the church and churchyard, and 400 took the castle. The Elector Palatine's forces pursued Geyer, and a column of 1,200 men captured the village and set fire to the church. Those who did not perish in the flames were slaughtered. The Elector's troops then breached the dilapidated castle wall, and attempted to storm the fortress. Turned back twice by the peasants, who had taken cover behind an inner wall, they shot up the inner wall as well, and tried a third assault, which was successful. Half of Geyer's men were massacred, but Geyer managed to escape with the other 200. Their hiding place, however, was discovered the following day (Whit-Monday). The Elector Palatine's soldiers surrounded the woods in which they lay hidden, and slaughtered all of them. Only seventeen prisoners were taken during those two days. Again Florian Geyer fought his way out of the encirclement with a few of his most intrepid fighters and set out to join the Gaildorf peasants, who had again assembled a body of about 7,000 men. But upon his arrival he found them mostly dispersed by the crushing news from every side. He made a last attempt to assemble the peasants dispersed in the woods, but was surprised by enemy forces at Hall on June 9 and fell fighting.

Truchsess, who had sent word to besieged Frauenberg after the Königshofen victory, now marched towards Würzburg. The Council came to a secret understanding with him, so that on the night of June 7 the League army

Armed Franconian peasants

was allowed to surround the city where 5,000 peasants were stationed, and the following morning marched without a single shot through the gates opened by the Council. This betrayal of the Würzburg "honourables" caused the last troops of the Franconian peasants to be disarmed and all their leaders to be arrested. Truchsess immediately ordered 81 of them decapitated. The various Franconian princes arrived in Würzburg one after the other, and among them the Bishop of Würzburg himself, the Bishop of Bamberg and the Margrave of Brandenburg-Ansbach. The gracious lords distributed the roles among themselves. Truchsess marched with the Bishop of Bamberg, who presently broke the agreement concluded with his peasants and opened his land to the murderous hordes of the League army. Margrave Casimir devastated his own land. Deiningen was burned and numerous villages were pillaged or gutted. In every town the Margrave held a blood-thirsty court. He ordered eighteen rebels beheaded in Neustadt-on-the-Aisch and in Markt-Bürgel forty-three suffered a similar fate. From there he went to Rothenburg where the honourables had already made a counter-revolution and arrested Stephan von Menzingen. The Rothenburg petty burghers and plebeians now had to pay heavily for behaving so ambiguously towards the peasants, refusing them all help until the very last, insisting in their local narrow-minded egotism on the suppression of countryside crafts in favour of the city guilds, and only unwillingly giving up the city revenues flowing in from the feudal services of the peasants. The Margrave ordered sixteen of them executed, and Menzingen naturally first of all. The Bishop of Würzburg marched through his region in a similar manner, pillaging, ravaging and burning everything on his way. He had 256 rebels decapitated on this triumphal march, and upon returning to Würzburg crowned his handiwork by beheading thirteen more Würzburg rebels.

In the Mainz region the vicegerent, Bishop Wilhelm von Strassburg, restored order without resistance. He executed only four men. Rheingau, which had also been in revolt, but where everybody had long since come home, was eventually invaded by Frowin von Hutten, a cousin of Ulrich, and fully "pacified" by the execution of twelve ringleaders. Frankfurt, which also experienced considerable revolutionary unrest, was held in check first by the conciliatory attitude of the Council and later by recruited troops. In the Rhenish Palatinate eight thousand peasants had assembled anew after the Elector's breach of faith, and had again burned monasteries and castles, but the Archbishop of Trier came to the aid of the Marshal of Habern, and made short work of them on June 23 at Pfeddersheim. A series of atrocities (eighty-two were executed in Pfeddersheim alone) and the capture of Weissenburg on July 7 put an end to the insurrection.

Of all the peasant troops only two were still unvanquished: the Hegau-Black Forest Troop and that of Allgäu. Archduke Ferdinand had tried intriguing against both. Just as Margrave Casimir and other princes sought to utilise the insurrection to annex church lands and principalities, Ferdinand wished to use it for the aggrandisement of the House of Austria. He had negotiated with the Allgäu commander, Walter Bach, and with the Hegau commander, Hans Müller of Bulgenbach, with the aim of inducing the peasants to declare allegiance to Austria, but though both chiefs were venal, they could not talk their troops into anything more than an armistice between the Allgäu Troop and the Archbishop, and neutrality towards Austria.

Retreating from the Württemberg region, the *peasants of Hegau* destroyed a number of castles and gathered reinforcements in the provinces of the Margraviate of Baden. On May 13 they marched on Freiburg, bombarded it from May 18, and entered it with flying colours when the town capitulated on May 23. From there they moved towards Stockach and Radolfzell, and waged a prolonged but unsuccessful small war against the garrisons of those towns. The latter, together with the nobility and other surrounding towns, appealed to the Lake peasants for help in accordance with the Weingarten agreement. The former rebels of the Lake Troop rose, 5,000 strong, against their fellow confederates. The peasants were so narrow-minded and short-sighted that only 600 refused to fight, expressing their wish to join the Hegau peasants, and were massacred. The Hegau peasants themselves, persuaded by Hans Müller of Bulgenbach, who had sold himself to the enemy, lifted their siege. When Hans Müller ran away, they dispersed. The remainder entrenched themselves on the Hilzingen Steep, where they were beaten and annihilated on July 16 by troops that had in the meantime become available. The Swiss cities negotiated an agreement on behalf of the Hegau peasants, which, however, did not prevent the other side from capturing and beheading Hans Müller in Laufenburg, his betrayal notwithstanding. In Breisgau the town of Freiburg also deserted the peasant union (July 17) and sent troops against it, but due to the weakness of the princely force an agreement was reached here as elsewhere, known as the agreement of Offenburg[1] (September 18), which also applied to Sundgau. The eight Black Forest groups and the Klettgau peasants, who were not as yet disarmed, were again compelled to rebel by the tyranny of Count von Sulz, and were repulsed in October. On November 13 the Black Forest peasants were forced to make an agreement,[2] and Waldshut, the last bulwark of the insurrection in the Upper Rhine, fell on December 6.

After Truchsess' departure the *Allgäu peasants* renewed their campaign against the monasteries and castles and wreaked vengeance for the ravages caused by the League army. They were confronted by few troops, which braved only insignificant isolated skirmishes and never followed them into the woods. In June, a movement against the honourables broke out in Memmingen, which had hitherto

---

[1] The Offenburg agreement concluded by the Breisgau insurgents with the Austrian Government stipulated restoration of former peasant services and the institution of harsh measures against peasant societies and "heretics". For its part, the government undertook to pardon rank-and-file members of the movement and confine itself to relatively modest fines. The amnesty, however, did not extend to the leaders of the uprising. But even this agreement, unfavourable to the peasants as it was, was soon faithlessly violated by the Austrian authorities and local feudal lords, who subjected the insurgents to bloody reprisals as soon as the latter laid down their arms.—*Ed.*

[2] By this agreement the Black Forest peasants were compelled to repeat their oath of allegiance to the Hapsburgs and to resume their former feudal services. They also undertook not to interfere with the bloody reprisals of the victors against the town of Waldshut, headquarters of the movement. The defenders of Waldshut, however, stood their ground for several weeks, and the town fell only due to the treachery of the burghers.—*Ed.*

been more or less neutral. This movement was defeated only due to the accidental presence in the vicinity of some League troops, who came in time to aid the honourables. Schappeler, preacher and leader of the plebeian movement, took refuge in St. Gallen. The peasants appeared before the town and were about to open fire and breach its wall when they learned that Truchsess was approaching from Würzburg. On June 27 they set out against him in two columns across Babenhausen and Obergünzburg. Archduke Ferdinand again attempted to win the peasants over to the House of Austria. On the strength of the armistice concluded with them, he demanded of Truchsess to march no farther against them. The Swabian League, however, ordered Truchsess to attack them, but to refrain from pillaging and burning. Truchsess, however, was too clever to relinquish his prime and most effective weapon, even if he were able to keep in check the lansquenets whom he had led from ·Lake Constance to the Main, from one atrocity to another. The peasants, numbering about 23,000, took up battle positions across the Iller and Leubas. Truchsess opposed them with 11,000. The positions of both armies were very strong. The cavalry was ineffective for the terrain that lay ahead, and if the Truchsess lansquenets were superior to the peasants in organisation, ammunition and discipline, the Allgäu peasants had in their ranks a host of former soldiers and experienced commanders, and possessed numerous well-manned cannons. On July 19 the League army opened fire, which was continued on both sides through July 20, but without any result. On July 21 Georg von Frundsberg joined Truchsess with 300 lansquenets. He knew many of the peasant commanders, for they had served under him in the Italian military expeditions, and entered into negotiations with them. Treason succeeded where military resources proved insufficient. Walter Bach and several other commanders and artillerymen sold themselves. They set fire to the powder stores of the peasants and induced the troop to attempt an enveloping movement, but as soon as the peasants left their strong positions they ran into an ambush, engineered by Truchsess in collusion with Bach and the other traitors. They were less capable of defending themselves since their traitorous commanders had left them under the pretext of reconnoitring and were already on their way to Switzerland. Thus, two of the peasant columns were routed, while a third, under Knopf of Leubas, was able to withdraw in good order. It resumed its position on the mountain of Kollen near Kempten, where it was surrounded by Truchsess. But the latter did not dare to attack the peasants; he cut off their supply routes and tried to demoralise them by burning about 200 villages in the vicinity. Hunger and the sight of their burning homes finally brought the peasants to their knees (July 25). More than twenty were immediately executed. Knopf of Leubas, the only leader of this troop who did not betray his banner, fled to Bregenz. There he was captured and hanged after a long imprisonment.

This brought the Peasant War in Swabia and Franconia to an end.

VI

Directly after the outbreak of the first movement in Swabia, *Thomas Münzer* again hurried to *Thuringia*, and in late February or early March stayed in the free imperial town of Mühlhausen, where his party was stronger than elsewhere. He held the threads of the whole movement and knew that a storm was brewing in Southern Germany. So he undertook to turn Thuringia into the centre of the movement in Northern Germany. He found the soil extremely fertile for it. Thuringia itself, the main scene of the Reformation movement, was in great ferment. The want of the downtrodden peasants and the prevailing revolutionary, religious and political doctrines had also made a general uprising imminent in the neighbouring provinces of Hesse, Saxony, and the Harz region. In Mühlhausen itself the bulk of the petty burgherdom was won over to the extreme Münzer doctrine and could hardly wait for the moment when it would assert its superiority over the haughty honourables. To prevent premature action, Münzer was compelled to appear in the role of moderator, but his disciple, Pfeifer, who held the reins of the movement there, had committed himself so greatly that he could not hold back the outbreak, and as early as March 17,

1525, before the general uprising in Southern Germany, Mühlhausen made its revolution. The old patrician Council was overthrown and the government handed over to the newly elected "eternal council", with Münzer as president.[1]

The worst thing that can befall a leader of an extreme party is to be compelled to take over a government at a time when society is not yet ripe for the domination of the class he represents and for the measures which that domination implies. What he *can* do depends not upon his will but upon the degree of antagonism between the various classes, and upon the level of development of the material means of existence, of the conditions of production and commerce upon which class contradictions always repose. What he *ought* to do, what his party demands of him, again depends not upon him or the stage of development of the class struggle and its conditions. He is bound to the doctrines and demands hitherto propounded which, again, do not proceed from the class relations of the moment, or from the more or less accidental level of production and commerce, but from his more or less penetrating insight into the general result of the social and political movement. Thus, he necessarily finds himself in an unsolvable dilemma. What he *can* do contradicts all his previous actions and principles, and the immediate interests of his party, and what he *ought* to do cannot be done. In a word, he is compelled to represent not his party or his class, but the class for whose domination the movement is then ripe. In the interests of the movement he is compelled to advance the interests of an alien class, and to feed his own class with talk and promises, and with the asseveration that the interests of that alien class are their own interests. He who is put into this awkward position is irrevocably lost. We have seen examples of this in recent times, and need only to recall the position taken in the last French provisional government by the representatives of the

---

[1] Later investigators determined that Münzer held no official post in the Mühlhausen "eternal council". But his presence at its sittings and his advice made him the virtual head of the new revolutionary government.—*Ed.*

proletariat,[1] though they themselves represented only a very low stage of development of the proletariat. Whoever can still speculate with official posts after the experiences of the February government—to say nothing of our own noble German provisional governments and imperial regencies[2]—is either foolish beyond measure or is only paying lip service to the extreme revolutionary party.

Münzer's position at the head of the "eternal council" of Mühlhausen was indeed much more precarious than that of any modern revolutionary regent. Not only the movement of his time, but the age was not ripe for the ideas of which he himself had only a faint notion. The class which he represented was still in its birth throes. It was not yet capable of assuming leadership over, and transforming, society. The social changes that his fancy evoked had little ground in the then existing economic conditions. What is more, these conditions were paving the way for a social system that was diametrically opposite to what he aspired to. Nevertheless, he was bound to his early sermon of Christian equality and evangelical community of ownership, and was compelled at least to attempt its realisation. Community of ownership, universal and equal labour, and abolition of all rights to exercise authority were proclaimed. But in reality Mühlhausen remained a republican imperial city with a somewhat democratised constitution, a senate elected by universal suffrage and controlled by a forum, and with a hastily improvised system of care for the poor. The social upheaval that so horrified its Protestant burgher contemporaries actually never transcended a feeble,

---

[1] Engels refers to the petty-bourgeois socialists, Louis Blanc and Alexander Marten (Albert), who represented the proletariat in the bourgeois provisional government of the French Republic instituted in February 1848. Cf. K. Marx and F. Engels, *Selected Works,* Moscow, 1962, Vol. I, pp. 118-228.—*Ed.*

[2] *Imperial regency*—the regent council of five established in June 1849 by the Frankfurt National Assembly pending enforcement of the "imperial constitution" framed by the Assembly, and the election of a German Emperor. This council, composed of "Left-wing" petty-bourgeois representatives, turned out to be just as cowardly, helpless, and incapable of revolutionary action as the Assembly itself. It was soon ignominiously dissolved.—*Ed.*

unconscious and premature attempt to establish the bourgeois society of a later period.

Münzer himself seems to have sensed the abyss between his theories and the surrounding realities, an abyss that he must have felt the more keenly, the more his visionary aspirations were distorted in the crude minds of his mass of followers. He devoted himself to extending and organising the movement with a zeal rare even for him. He wrote letters and sent messengers and emissaries in all directions. His writings and sermons breathed a revolutionary fanaticism, astonishing even when compared with his former works. The naïve youthful humour of Münzer's pre-revolutionary pamphlets is gone. The placid scholastic language of the thinker, typical of his earlier years, is gone too. Münzer becomes a positive prophet of the revolution. He untiringly fans the hatred against the ruling classes, he spurs the wildest passions, and uses only the forceful language that religious and nationalist delirium put into the mouths of the Old Testament prophets. The style he adopts reflects the educational level of the public he seeks to influence.

The example of Mühlhausen and Münzer's propaganda had a rapid and far-reaching effect. In *Thuringia, Eichsfeld*, the *Harz*, the *duchies of Saxony*, in *Hesse* and *Fulda*, in *Upper Franconia* and in *Vogtland*, the peasants arose, assembled in armies, and set fire to castles and monasteries. Münzer was recognised more or less as the leader of the entire movement, and Mühlhausen remained its centre, while a purely burgher movement won out in Erfurt and the ruling party there acted ambiguously towards the peasants.

The princes in Thuringia were at first just as perplexed and helpless against the peasants as they had been in Franconia and Swabia. Only in the last days of April did the Landgrave of Hesse succeed in assembling a corps. It was the same Landgrave Philip, whose piety is praised so much by the Protestant and bourgeois histories of the Reformation, and of whose infamies against the peasants we shall presently have a word to say. By a series of quick movements and decisive actions, Landgrave Philip subdued the major part of his land, called up new contingents, and then turned into the region of the Abbot of Fulda, who had hitherto been his feudal lord. On May 3 he defeated the Fulda peasant troop at Frauenberg, subdued the whole land, and seized the opportunity not only of freeing himself from the sovereignty of the Abbot, but of making the Abbey of Fulda a vassalage of Hesse, pending, naturally, its subsequent secularisation. He then took Eisenach and Langensalza, and advanced against Mühlhausen, the headquarters of the rebellion, jointly with the ducal Saxon troops. Münzer assembled his forces, comprising 8,000 men and several cannons, at Frankenhausen. The Thuringian troop had little of the fighting power which a part of the Upper Swabian and Franconian troops developed in their struggle with Truchsess. It was poorly armed and badly disciplined; it had few ex-soldiers in its ranks, and lacked sorely in leadership. It appears, Münzer himself had no military knowledge. All the same, the princes thought it best to use the same tactics against him that so often helped Truchsess to victory: breach of faith. They launched negotiations on May 16, concluded an armistice, and then suddenly attacked the peasants before the armistice elapsed.

Münzer stationed his people on the mountain still called Schlachtberg (Mount Battle), behind a barricade of wagons. Discouragement was spreading rapidly among his men. The princes promised them indulgence if they would deliver Münzer alive. Münzer called a general assembly to debate the princes' proposals. A knight and a priest spoke in favour of capitulation. Münzer had them both brought inside the circle and decapitated. This act of terrorist energy, jubilantly met by resolute revolutionaries, instilled certain order among the troop, but most of the men would have gone away in the end without resistance, had it not been noticed that the princes' lansquenets, who had encircled the mountain, were approaching in closed columns in spite of the armistice. A front was hurriedly formed behind the wagons, but already cannon and rifle balls were showering upon the practically defenseless peasants, unaccustomed to battle, and the lansquenets had reached the barricade. After a brief resistance the line of wagons was breached, the peasant cannons captured, and the peasants dispersed. They fled in wild disorder to fall into the hands of the enveloping columns and the cavalry, who staged an appalling massacre. Out of 8,000 peasants over 5,000 were slaughtered. The survivors arrived at Frankenhausen, and the princes' cavalry came hot on their heels. The city was taken. Münzer, wounded in the head, was discovered in a house and taken prisoner. On May 25 Mühlhausen also surrendered. Pfeifer, who had remained there, escaped, but was captured in the region of Eisenach.

Münzer was put on the rack in the presence of the princes, and then decapitated. He went to his death with the same courage with which he had lived. He was at most twenty-eight when executed. Pfeifer was also executed, and many others besides. In Fulda, Philip of Hesse, that holy man, opened his bloody court. He and the Saxon princes had many others killed by the sword, among them in Eisenach, twenty-four; in Langensalza, forty-one; after the battle of Frankenhausen, 300; in Mühlhausen, more than 100; at Görmar, twenty-six; at Tüngeda, fifty; at Sangerhausen, twelve; in Leipzig, eight, not to speak of mutilations and more moderate measures, pillaging and burning villages and towns.

Mühlhausen was compelled to give up its imperial liberty, and was incorporated in the Saxon lands, just as the Abbey of Fulda was incorporated in the Landgraviate of Hesse.

The princes now marched through the forest of Thuringia, where Franconian peasants of the Bildhausen camp had joined the Thuringians and had burned many castles. A battle took place outside Meiningen. The peasants were beaten and withdrew towards the town, which suddenly closed its gates to them and threatened to attack them from the rear. The troop thrown into confusion by this betrayal, surrendered to the princes and ran off in all directions while negotiations were still under way. The Bildhausen troop had long since dispersed, and after its defeat the remaining insurgents of Saxony, Hesse, Thuringia and Upper Franconia were annihilated.

In *Alsace* the rebellion broke out later than on the right bank of the Rhine. The peasants of the bishopric of Strassburg rose up as late as the middle of April. Soon after, there was an uprising of peasants in Upper Alsace and Sundgau. On April 18 a contingent of Lower Alsace peasants pillaged the monastery of Altdorf. Other troops formed near Ebersheim and Barr, as well as in the Willer and Urbis valleys. These amalgamated into a large Lower Alsace troop and seized towns and hamlets and destroyed monasteries. Everywhere one out of every three men was called to serve in the troop. The Twelve Articles of this group were much more radical than those of the Swabian and Franconian.[1]

While one column of Lower Alsatians concentrated near St. Hippolite early in May, and after a futile attempt to take that town occupied Bercken on May 10, Rappoltsweiler on May 13, and Reichenweier on May 14 by an understanding with their citizenry, a second column under Erasmus Gerber moved in for a surprise attack on Strassburg. The attempt failed, and the column now turned towards the Vosges, destroyed the monastery of Mauersmünster and besieged Zabern, which surrendered on May 13. From here it moved towards the Lorraine frontier and roused the adjacent section of the duchy, at the same time fortifying the mountain passes. Two big camps were formed at Herbitzheim on the Saar, and at Neuburg. Nearly four thousand German-Lorraine peasants entrenched themselves at Saargemünd. Finally, two advanced troops, the Kolben troop in the Vosges at Stürzelbronn, and the Kleeburg troop at Weissenburg, covered the front and the right flank, while the left flank adjoined the Upper Alsatians.

The latter, on the march since April 20, had forced Sulz into the peasant fraternity on May 10, Gebweiler on May 12, and Sennheim and its vicinity on May 15. The Austrian government and the surrounding imperial towns united against them, but were too weak to offer serious resistance,

---

[1] The Articles of the Alsatian peasants not only defined more sharply the anti-feudal demands of the "Twelve Articles" of the Swabian-Franconian peasantry (abolition of serfdom, return of common lands usurped by the nobility, etc.), but in many respects went farther than they. They were also directed against usurers (the clause on the abolition of usurers' interest rates, and others), they demanded the abolition not only of the small, but of the great tithe as well, proclaimed the right of the local population to depose officials who aroused the dissatisfaction of the people and to replace them with others.—*Ed*.

Foot and mounted revolutionary peasants

not to speak of attacking. Thus, the whole of Alsace, with the exception of a few towns, fell into the hands of the insurgents by the middle of May.

But the army that was to break the wanton spirit of the Alsatians was already approaching. It was the *French* who here restored the power of the nobility. On May 6 Duke Anton of Lorraine marched out with an army of 30,000, among them the flower of the French nobility, as well as Spanish, Piedmontese, Lombardic, Greek and Albanian auxiliary troops. On May 16 he engaged 4,000 peasants at Lupstein, whom he defeated without effort, and on May 17 he forced Zabern, which was occupied by the peasants, to surrender. But even while the Lorrainers were entering the city and the peasants were being disarmed, the conditions of the surrender were broken. The defenseless peasants were attacked by the lansquenets, and most of them were slain. The remaining Lower Alsace columns disbanded, and Duke Anton went on to meet the Upper Alsatians. The latter, who had refused to reinforce the Lower Alsatians at Zabern, were now attacked at Scherweiler by the entire force of Lorrainers. They put up a plucky fight, but the enormous numerical superiority of 30,000, against 7,000, and the betrayal of a number of knights, especially that of the magistrate of Reichenweier, made all daring futile. They were beaten and dispersed to the last man. The Duke now proceeded to subdue the whole of Alsace with the usual cruelty. Only Sundgau was spared his presence. By threatening to call him into the land, the Austrian government induced the peasants to conclude the Ensisheim agreement early in June. But it broke the agreement very soon and hanged the preachers and leaders of the movement en masse. The peasants rebelled anew, and Sundgau was finally drawn into the Offenburg agreement (September 18).

It now remains only to describe the Peasant War in the *Alpine regions of Austria*. These regions and the adjoining *Archbishopric of Salzburg* had been in continuous opposition to the government and the nobility ever since the Stara Prawa, and the Reformation doctrines found there a fertile soil. Religious persecution and arbitrary oppressive taxation precipitated the rebellion.

The city of *Salzburg*, supported by peasants and pitmen, had been in conflict with the Archbishop since 1522 over its city privileges and religious practices. Late in 1524 the Archbishop attacked the city with recruited lansquenets, terrorised it with the cannons of the castle, and persecuted the heretical preachers. At the same time he imposed new crushing taxes and thereby irritated the population to the extreme. In the spring of 1525, simultaneously with the Swabian-Franconian and Thuringian uprisings, the peasants and pitmen of the whole country suddenly rose up in arms, organised under the commanders *Prassler* and *Weitmoser*, liberated the city and besieged the castle of Salzburg. Like the West-German peasants, they organised a Christian Alliance and formulated their demands in articles, of which they had fourteen.[1]

In *Styria*, *Upper Austria*, *Carinthia* and *Carniola*, where new extortionate taxes, duties and edicts had severely injured the basic interests of the people, the peasants arose in the spring of 1525. They took a number of castles and at Goyss defeated Dietrichstein, the old field commander and the conqueror of the Stara Prawa. Although the government succeeded in placating some of the insurgents with false promises, the bulk of them stayed together and united with the Salzburg peasants, so that the entire region of Salzburg and the major part of Upper Austria, Styria, Carinthia and Carniola were in the hands of the peasants and pitmen.

In the Tirol the Reformation doctrines had also found numerous adherents. Münzer's emissaries had been successfully active here, even more so than in the other Alpine regions of Austria. Archduke Ferdinand persecuted the preachers of the new doctrine as elsewhere, and impinged upon the rights of the population by arbitrary financial regulations. The result, as everywhere, was an uprising that broke out in the spring of 1525. The insurgents, commanded by Geismaier, a Münzer man, who was the only mili-

---

[1] Their articles, in the main, reproduced the demands of the "Twelve Articles" of the Swabian and Franconian peasants (abolition of serfdom, the small tithe, the death duty and other feudal duties, and election of priests, etc.). In addition, they contained certain demands of a local nature.—*Ed.*

tary talent of any significance among all the peasant chiefs, took a great number of castles, and carried on energetically against the priests, particularly in the south in the Etsch region. The Vorarlberg peasants also arose and joined the Allgäu peasants.

The Archbishop, hard-pressed from all sides, now began to make concession after concession to the rebels whom a short time before he had wished to annihilate by fire, pillage and murder. He summoned the diets of the hereditary lands and, pending their opening, concluded an armistice with the peasants. In the meantime he was arming for all he was worth, so he could shortly speak to the blasphemers in a different tongue.

Naturally, the armistice was not long observed. Dietrichstein, having run short of cash, began to levy contributions in the duchies; his Slavic and Magyar troops indulged in the most shameless cruelty against the population. This incited the Styrians to a new revolt. The peasants attacked Dietrichstein at Schladming on the night of July 2, and slaughtered everybody who did not speak German. Dietrichstein himself was captured. On the morning of July 3 the peasants called a jury and sentenced to death forty Czech and Croatian nobles among their prisoners. They were beheaded on the spot. That had its effect; the Archduke immediately consented to all the demands of the Estates of the five duchies (Upper and Lower Austria, Styria, Carinthia and Carniola).

The demands of the Landtag were also granted in Tirol, and the North was thereby pacified. The South, however, stood firm on its original demands, scorning the much more moderate decisions of the Landtag, and remained under arms. Only in December was the Archduke able to restore order by force. He did not fail to execute a great number of instigators and leaders of the upheaval who fell into his hands.

Ten thousand Bavarians moved in August against Salzburg under Georg von Frundsberg. This impressive show of strength, and the quarrels that broke out in their ranks, induced the Salzburg peasants to conclude an agreement with the Archbishop on September 1, which was also accepted by the Archduke. However, the two princes, who had meanwhile considerably strengthened their troops, soon broke the agreement and thereby compelled the Salzburg peasants to start a new uprising. The insurgents held their own throughout the winter. In the spring Geismaier came to them and launched a splendid campaign against the troops approaching from every side. In a series of brilliant battles in May and June 1526, he successively defeated the Bavarian, Austrian and Swabian League troops and the lansquenets of the Archbishop of Salzburg, and for long prevented the various corps from uniting. He also found time to besiege Radstadt. Surrounded finally by superior forces, he was compelled to withdraw, and fought his way out of the encirclement, leading the remnants of his troop across the Austrian Alps into Venetian territory. The Republic of Venice and Switzerland served the indefatigable peasant chief as starting points for new intrigues. For a whole year he made attempts to involve them in a war with Austria, which would have given him an opportunity to begin a new peasant uprising. The hand of an assassin reached him, however, in the course of these negotiations. Archduke Ferdinand and the Archbishop of Salzburg could not rest as long as Geismaier was alive. They hired an assassin who succeeded in ending the life of the dangerous rebel in 1527.

VII

The epilogue of the Peasant War closed with Geismaier's withdrawal into Venetian territory. The peasants were everywhere brought back under the sway of their ecclesiastical, noble or patrician overlords. The agreements that were here and there concluded with them were broken and the heavy burdens augmented by the enormous indemnities imposed by the victors on the vanquished. The most magnificent revolutionary effort of the German people ended in ignominious defeat and, for the time being, in redoubled oppression. In the long run, however, the situation of the peasants did not deteriorate on account of the suppression of the uprising. Whatever the nobility, princes and priests could wring out of the peasants year in and year out, had been wrung out even before the war.

The German peasant of that day has this in common with the present-day proletarian that his share in the products of labour was limited to a subsistence minimum necessary for his maintenance and the propagation of the peasant race. On the whole, nothing more could be got out of the peasants. True, the more prosperous middle peasants were ruined, hosts of bondsmen were forced into serfdom, whole stretches of community land were confiscated, and a great many peasants were made destitute or forced to become tramps or city plebeians by the destruction of their homes, the devastation of their fields and the general disorder. But war and devastation were everyday phenomena at that time and, in general, the peasant class was at too low a level for increased taxation to cause any lasting deterioration of its wretched state. The subsequent religious wars, and, finally, the Thirty Years' War with its recurrent general devastation and depopulation struck the peasants much more painfully than the Peasant War. It was notably the Thirty Years' War which destroyed the most important part of the productive forces in agriculture, through which, as well as through the simultaneous destruction of many towns, the peasants, plebeians and ruined burghers were reduced to a state of Irish misery in its worst form.

The class that suffered most from the Peasant War was the *clergy*. Its monasteries and endowments were burned; its treasures were plundered, sold abroad, or melted down, and its stores were consumed. It was everywhere least capable of resistance, and yet it was the main target of the people's wrath. The other Estates—princes, nobles and burghers—even experienced a secret joy at the distress of the hated prelates. The Peasant War had made popular the idea of secularising the church estates in favour of the peasants. The lay princes, and partly the towns, determined to secularise the estates for *their own* good, and soon the possessions of the prelates in Protestant regions were in the hands of the princes, or the honourables. But the power of the ecclesiastical princes was also impaired, and the lay princes knew how to exploit the people's hatred in this respect. We have seen, for instance, how the Abbot of Fulda was relegated from a feudal lord to the vassal of Philip of Hesse. The town of Kempten forced its prince-abbot to sell it a number of precious privileges, which he enjoyed in the town, for a ridiculous trifle.

The *nobility* had also suffered considerably. Most of its castles were destroyed and some of its most respected families were ruined and could find a living only in the service of the princes. Its weakness in face of the peasantry was proved. It had been beaten everywhere, and had been forced to surrender. Only the armies of the princes had saved it. The nobility was bound more and more to lose its significance as an Estate under the Empire, and to fall under the dominion of the princes.

Nor did the *towns* generally gain anything from the Peasant War. The rule of the honourables was almost everywhere re-established; the burgher opposition was broken for a long time. The old patrician routine dragged on in this way, tying commerce and industry hand and foot, up to the time of the French Revolution. Moreover, the towns were made responsible by the princes for the momentary successes which the burgher or plebeian parties achieved within their confines during the struggle. The towns that had even previously belonged to princely estates had to pay heavy indemnities, to give up their privileges, and were put under the avaricious rule of the princes (Frankenhausen, Arnstadt, Schmalkalden, Würzburg, etc.). Towns of the Empire were incorporated into the territories of the princes (Mühlhausen, for example), or at least made morally dependent on the neighbouring princes, as was the case with many imperial towns in Franconia.

Under the circumstances, the *princes* alone gained from the Peasant War. We have seen at the very beginning of our account that the low level of industry, commerce and agriculture ruled out any centralisation of Germans into a *nation*, that it allowed only local and provincial centralisation, and that the princes, representatives of centralisation within disruption, were the only Estate to profit from all the changes in the existing social and political conditions. The development of Germany in that day was so low and at the same time so dissimilar in the various provinces, that alongside the lay principalities there could still exist ecclesiastical sovereignties, city republics, and sovereign counts and barons. Simultaneously, however, this development was continually, though slowly and feebly, pressing towards *provincial* centralisation, i.e., towards the subordination of all the other imperial Estates to the princes. That is why only the princes could have gained from the outcome of the Peasant War. And that is exactly what happened. They gained not only relatively, through the weakening of their opponents—the clergy, nobility and the towns, but also absolutely, in that they carried off the *spolia opima* (the main spoils) of all the other Estates. The church estates were secularised in their favour; part of the nobility, fully or partly ruined, was obliged gradually to accept vassalage; the indemnities of the towns and peasant communities swelled their treasuries, and, furthermore, the abolition of so many town privileges now gave much greater play to their favourite financial operations.

German disunity, whose spread and intensification was the chief result of the Peasant War, was, at the same time, the cause of its failure.

We have seen that Germany was split not only into numberless independent, almost totally alien provinces, but that in every one of these provinces the nation was broken up into a multifold structure of Estates and fractions of Estates. Besides princes and priests we find nobles and peasants in the countryside, and in the towns we find patricians, burghers and plebeians, whose interests as Estates differed radically, even where they did not cross each other or come into conflict. Besides all these complicated interests there were still the interests of the Emperor and the Pope. We have seen how ponderously, imperfectly, and how differently in the various localities, all these interests finally formed three major groups. We have seen that in spite of this painful grouping each Estate opposed the line indicated by circumstances for the national development, that each Estate acted on its own, coming into conflict not only with the conservative, but also with the other opposition Estates, and that it was bound to fail in the end. That was the fate of the nobility in Sickingen's uprising, that of the peasants in the Peasant War, and of the burghers in all of their insipid Reformation. Thus, even the peasants and plebeians in most parts of Germany failed to unite for joint action and stood in each other's way. We have also seen the causes of this fractionisation of the class struggle and the resultant total defeat of the revolutionary, and partial defeat of the burgher, movements.

How local and provincial separatism and the resultant local and provincial narrow-mindedness ruined the whole movement, how neither burghers, nor peasants, nor ple-

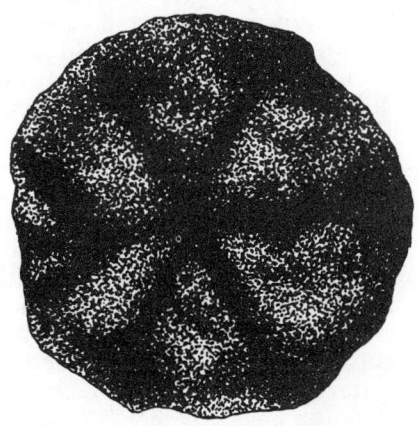

The peasants' stamp, secret identity sign of the revolutionary peasants

beians could unite for concerted national action; how the peasants of every province acted only for themselves, as a rule refusing aid to the insurgent peasants of the neighbouring regions, and were, consequently, annihilated in separate battles one after another by armies which in most cases were hardly one-tenth the total number of the insurgent masses—all this should be clear enough from this account. The various armistices and agreements concluded by individual troops with their adversaries represent just as many acts of betrayal of the common cause. The only possible grouping of the various troops not according to the greater or smaller singleness of their own actions, but according to the singleness of the particular adversary to whom they succumbed, is most striking proof of the degree of mutual alienation of the peasants in the various provinces.

Here also the analogy with the movement of 1848-50 leaps to the eye. In 1848, as in the Peasant War, the interests of the opposition classes conflicted and each acted on its own. The bourgeoisie, much too developed to suffer any longer the feudal and bureaucratic absolutism, was, however, not as yet powerful enough to subordinate the claims of other classes to its own interests. The proletariat, much too weak to count on a rapid passage through the bourgeois period and on an immediate conquest of power, had already learned too well under absolutism the honeyed sweetness of the bourgeois regime and was generally far too developed to identify for even a moment its own emancipation with that of the bourgeoisie. The bulk of the nation—petty burghers, owners of workshops (artisans), and peasants—was left in the lurch by its currently natural ally, the bourgeoisie, because it was too revolutionary, and partly by the proletariat, because it was not sufficiently advanced. Divided in itself the bourgeoisie achieved nothing, while opposing fellow opponents on the Right and Left. As to provincial narrow-mindedness, it could hardly have been greater among the peasants in 1525 than it was among the classes participating in the movement of 1848. The hundred local revolutions as well as the attendant and unhindered hundred local reactions, survival of the separation of numerous small states, etc., etc.—all this is eloquent testimony indeed. *He who still dreams of a federated republic after the two German revolutions of 1525 and 1848, and their results, belongs in the insane asylum.*

Still, the two revolutions, that of the sixteenth century and that of 1848-50, are, in spite of all analogies, essentially different. The revolution of 1848 speaks for the progress of Europe, if not of Germany.

Who profited by the Revolution of 1525? The *princes*. Who profited by the Revolution of 1848? The *big* princes, Austria and Prussia. Behind the minor princes of 1525 stood the petty burghers, who chained the princes to themselves by taxes. Behind the big princes of 1850, behind Austria and Prussia, there stand the modern big bourgeois, rapidly getting them under their yoke by means of the national debt. And behind the big bourgeois stand the proletarians.

The revolution of 1525 was a domestic German affair. The English, French, Bohemians and Hungarians had already gone through their peasant wars when the Germans began theirs. If Germany was disunited, Europe was much more so. As for the revolution of 1848, it was not a domestic German affair, and was an episode in a great European movement. Its motive forces throughout its duration transcended the narrow limits of one country, and even those of one part of the world. In fact, the countries which were the arena of revolution were least active in producing it. They were more or less unconscious and hesitant raw material, moulded in the course of the movement in which the entire world participates today, a movement which under existing social conditions may appear to us only as an alien power but which, in the end, is nothing but our own. This is why the revolution of 1848-50 cannot end in the way the revolution of 1525 ended.

Written by F. Engels in the summer of 1850

First printed in the *Neue Rheinische Zeitung. Politisch-ökonomische Revue,* No. 5-6, 1850

Published in separate editions in 1870 and 1875 in Leipzig with a preface by F. Engels

The translation is of the third German edition of 1875. Misprints of dates, geographical and proper names have been corrected

APPENDIX

I

F. ENGELS

THE MARK[1]

In a country like Germany, in which quite half the population live by agriculture, it is necessary that the socialist working-men, and through them the peasants, should learn how the present system of landed property, large as

---

[1] *The Mark* was published by Engels as an appendix to the German edition of *Socialism: Utopian and Scientific* (1882). In 1883 it was reprinted in *Der Sozial-Demokrat,* the central organ of the German Social-Democrats, and was also published as a separate pamphlet. In his introduction to the English-language edition of *Socialism: Utopian and Scientific,* which appeared in 1892, Engels wrote: "The appendix, *The Mark,* was written with the intention of spreading among the German Socialist Party some elementary knowledge of the history and development of landed property in Germany. This seemed all the more necessary at a time when the assimilation by that party of the working people of the towns was in a fair way of completion, and when the agricultural labourers and peasants had to be taken in hand. This appendix has been included in the translation, as the original forms of tenure of land common to all Teutonic tribes, and the history of their decay, are even less known in England than in Germany. I have left the text as it stands in the original, without alluding to the hypothesis recently started by Maxim Kovalevsky, according to which the partition of the arable and meadow lands among the members of the Mark was preceded by their being cultivated for joint-account by a large patriarchal family community embracing several generations (as exemplified by the still existing South Slavonian Zadruga), and that the partition, later on, took place when the community had increased, so as to become too unwieldly for joint-account management. Kovalevsky is probably quite right, but the matter is still *sub judice*." (K. Marx and F. Engels, *Selected Works,* Vol. II, Moscow, 1962, p. 95.)—*Ed.*

well as small, has arisen. It is necessary to contrast the misery of the agricultural labourers of the present time and the mortgage-servitude of the small peasants, with the old common property of all free men in what was then in truth their "fatherland", the free common possession of all by inheritance. I shall give, therefore, a short historical sketch of the primitive agrarian conditions of the German tribes. A few traces of these have survived until our own time, but all through the Middle Ages they served as the basis and as the type of all public institutions, and permeated the whole of public life, not only in Germany, but also in the north of France, England, and Scandinavia. And yet they have been so completely forgotten, that recently G. L. Maurer has had to rediscover their real significance.

Two fundamental facts, that arose spontaneously, govern the primitive history of all, or of almost all, nations; the grouping of the people according to kindred, and common property in the soil. And this was the case with the Germans. As they had brought with them from Asia the method of grouping by tribes and gentes, as they even in the time of the Romans so drew up their battle array, that those related to each other always stood shoulder to shoulder, this grouping also governed the partitioning of their new territory east of the Rhine and north of the Danube. Each tribe settled down upon the new possession, not according to whim or accident, but, as Cæsar expressly states, according to the gens-relationship between the members of the tribe. A particular area was apportioned to each of the nearly related larger groups, and on this again the individual gentes, each including a certain number of families, settled down by villages. A number of allied villages formed a hundred (old high German, *huntari*; old Norse, *heradh*). A number of hundreds formed a *gau* or shire. The sum total of the shires was the people itself. The land which was not taken possession of by the village remained at the disposal of the hundred. What was not assigned to the latter remained for the shire. Whatever after that was still to be disposed of—generally a very large tract of land—was the immediate possession of the whole people. Thus in Sweden we find all these different stages of common holding side by side. Each village had its village common land (*bys almänningar*), and beyond this was the hundred common land (*härads*), the shire common land (*lands*), and finally the people's common land. This last, claimed by the king as representative of the whole nation, was known therefore as *konungs almänningar*. But all of these, even the royal lands, were named, without distinction, *almänningar*, common land.

This old Swedish arrangement of the common land, in its minute subdivision, evidently belongs to a later stage of development. If it ever did exist in Germany, it soon vanished. The rapid increase in the population led to the establishment of a number of daughter-villages on the *Mark.*, i.e., on the large tract of land attributed to each individual mother-village. These daughter-villages formed a single mark-association with the mother-village, on the basis of equal or of restricted rights. Thus we find everywhere in Germany, so far as research goes back, a larger or smaller number of villages united in *one* mark-association. But these associations were, at least at first, still subject to the great federations of the marks of the hundred, or of the shire. And, finally, the people, as a whole, originally formed one single great mark-association, not only for the administration of the land that remained the immediate possession of the people, but also as a supreme court over the subordinate local marks.

Until the time when the Frankish kingdom subdued Germany east of the Rhine, the centre of gravity of the mark-association seems to have been in the *gau* or shire— the shire seems to have formed the unit mark-association. For, upon this assumption alone is it explicable that, upon the official division of the kingdom, so many old and large marks reappear as shires. Soon after this time began the decay of the old large marks. Yet even in the code known as the *Kaiserrecht*, the "Emperor's Law" of the thirteenth or fourteenth century, it is a general rule that a mark includes from six to twelve villages.

In Cæsar's time a great part at least of the Germans, the Suevi, to wit, who had not yet got any fixed settlement, cultivated their fields in common. From analogy with other peoples we may take it that this was carried on in such a way that the individual gentes, each including a number of nearly related families, cultivated in common the land apportioned to them, which was changed from year to year, and divided the products among the families. But after the Suevi, about the beginning of our era, had settled down in their new domains, this soon ceased. At all events, Tacitus (150 years after Cæsar) only mentions the tilling of the soil by individual families. But the land to be tilled only belonged to these for a year. Every year it was divided up anew and redistributed.

How this was done is still to be seen at the present time on the Moselle and in the Hochwald, on the so-called "Gehöferschaften". There the whole of the land under cultivation, arable and meadows, not annually, it is true, but every three, six, nine, or twelve years, is thrown together and parcelled out into a number of "Gewanne", or areas, according to situation and the quality of the soil. Each Gewann is again divided into as many equal parts, long, narrow strips, as there are claimants in the association. These are shared by lot among the members, so that every member receives an equal portion in each Gewann. At the present time the shares have become unequal by divisions among heirs, sales, etc.; but the old full share still furnishes the unit that determines the half, or quarter, or one-eighth shares. The uncultivated land, forest and pasture land is still a common possession for common use.

The same primitive arrangement obtained until the beginning of this century in the so-called assignments by lot (Losgüter) of the Rhine palatinate in Bavaria, whose arable land has since been turned into the private property of individuals. The Gehöferschaften also find it more and more to their interest to let the periodical redivision become obsolete and to turn the changing ownership into settled private property. Thus most of them, if not all, have died out in the last forty years and given place to villages with peasant proprietors using the forests and pasture land in common.

The first piece of ground that passed into the private property of individuals was that on which the house stood. The inviolability of the dwelling, that basis of all personal freedom, was transferred from the caravan of the nomadic train to the log house of the stationary peasant, and gradually was transformed into a complete right of property in the homestead. This had already come about in the time of Tacitus. The free German's homestead must, even in that time, have been excluded from the mark, and thereby inaccessible to its officials, a safe place of refuge for fugitives, as we find it described in the regulations of the marks of later times, and to some extent, even in the "leges Barbarorum", the codifications of German tribal customary law, written down from the fifth to the eighth century. For the sacredness of the dwelling was not the effect but the cause of its transformation into private property.

Four or five hundred years after Tacitus, according to the same law-books, the cultivated land also was the hereditary, although not the absolute freehold property of individual peasants, who had the right to dispose of it by sale or any other means of transfer. The causes of this transformation, as far as we can trace them, are twofold.

First, from the beginning there were in Germany itself, besides the close villages already described, with their complete ownership in common of the land, other villages where, besides homesteads, the fields also were excluded from the mark, the property of the community, and were parcelled out among the individual peasants as their hereditary property. But this was only the case where the nature of the place, so to say, compelled it: in narrow valleys, as in the Berg region, and on narrow, flat ridges between marshes, as in Westphalia; later on, in the Odenwald, and in almost all the Alpine valleys. In these places the village consisted, as it does now, of scattered individual dwellings, each surrounded by the fields belonging to it. A periodical redivision of the arable land was in these cases hardly possible, and so what remained within the mark was only the circumjacent untilled land. When, later, the right to dispose of the homestead by transfer to a third person became an important consideration, those who were free owners of their fields found themselves in an advantageous position. The wish to attain these advantages may have led in many of the villages with common ownership of the land to letting the customary method of partition die out and to the transformation of the individual shares of the members into hereditary and transferable freehold property.

But, second, conquest led the Germans on to Roman territory, where, for centuries, the soil had been private property (the unlimited property of Roman law), and where the small number of conquerors could not possibly altogether do away with a form of holding so deeply rooted. The connection of hereditary private property in fields and meadows with Roman law, at all events on territory that had been Roman, is supported by the fact that such remains of common property in arable land as have come down to our time are found on the left bank of the Rhine, i.e., on conquered territory, but territory *thoroughly Germanised*. When the Franks settled here in the fifth century, common ownership in the fields must still have existed among them, otherwise we should not find there Gehöferschaften and Losgüter. But here also private ownership soon got the mastery, for this form of holding only do we find mentioned, insofar as arable land is concerned, in the riparian law of the sixth century. And in the interior of Germany, as I have said, the cultivated land also soon became private property.

But if the German conquerors adopted private ownership in fields and meadows, i.e., gave up at the first division of the land, or soon after, any repartition (for it was nothing more than this), they introduced, on the other hand, everywhere their German mark system, with common holding of woods and pastures, together with the overlordship of the mark in respect to the partitioned land. This happened not only with the Franks in the north of France and the Anglo-Saxons in England, but also with the Burgundians in Eastern France, the Visigoths in the south of France and Spain, and the Ostrogoths and Langobardians in Italy. In these last named countries, however, as far as is known, traces of the mark government have lasted until the present time almost exclusively in the higher mountain regions.

The form that the mark government has assumed after

the periodical partition of the cultivated land had fallen into disuse, is that which now meets us, not only in the old popular laws of the fifth, sixth, seventh, and eighth centuries, but also in the English and Scandinavian law-books of the Middle Ages, in the many German mark regulations (the so-called Weistümer) from the thirteenth to the seventeenth century, and in the customary laws (coûtumes) of Northern France.

Whilst the association of the mark gave up the right of, from time to time, partitioning fields and meadows anew among its individual members, it did not give up a single one of its other rights over these lands. And these rights were very important. The association had only transferred their fields to individuals with a view to their being used as arable and meadow land, and with that view alone. Beyond that the individual owner had no right. Treasures found in the earth, if they lay deeper than the ploughshare goes, did not, therefore originally belong to him, but to the community. It was the same thing with digging for ores, and the like. All these rights were, later on, stolen by the princes and landlords for their own use.

But, further, the use of arable and meadow lands was under the supervision and direction of the community and that in the following form. Wherever three-field farming obtained—and that was almost everywhere—the whole cultivated area of the village was divided into three equal parts, each of which was alternately sown one year with winter seed, the second with spring seed, and the third lay fallow. Thus the village had each year its winter field, its spring field, its fallow field. In the partition of the land care was taken that each member's share was made up of equal portions from each of the three fields, so that everyone could, without difficulty, accommodate himself to the regulations of the community, in accordance with which he would have to sow autumn seed only in his winter field, and so on.

The field whose turn it was to lie fallow returned, for the time being, into the common possession, and served the community in general for pasture. And as soon as the two other fields were reaped, they likewise became again common property until seed-time, and were used as common pasturage. The same thing occurred with the meadows after the aftermath. The owners had to remove the fences upon all fields given over to pasturage. This compulsory pasturage, of course, made it necessary that the time of sowing and of reaping should not be left to the individual, but be fixed for all by the community or by custom.

All other land, i.e., all that was not house and farmyard, or so much of the mark as had been distributed among individuals, remained, as in early times, common property for common use; forests, pasture lands, heaths, moors, rivers, ponds, lakes, roads and bridges, hunting and fishing grounds. Just as the share of each member in so much of the mark as was distributed was of equal size, so was his share also in the use of the "common mark". The nature of this use was determined by the members of the community as a whole. So, too, was the mode of partition, if the soil that had been cultivated no longer sufficed, and a portion of the common mark was taken under cultivation. The chief use of the common mark was in pasturage for the cattle and feeding of pigs on acorns. Besides that, the forest yielded timber and firewood, litter for the animals, berries and mushrooms, whilst the moor, where it existed, yielded turf. The regulations as to pasture, the use of wood, etc., make up the most part of the many mark records written down at various epochs between the thirteenth and the eighteenth centuries, at the time when the old unwritten law of custom began to be contested. The common woodlands that are still met with here and there, are the remnants of these ancient unpartitioned marks. Another relic, at all events in West and South Germany, is the idea, deeply rooted in the popular consciousness, that the forest should be common property, wherein everyone may gather flowers, berries, mushrooms, beechnuts and the like, and generally so long as he does no mischief, act and do as he will. But this also Bismarck remedies, and with his famous berry-legislation brings down the Western Provinces to the level of the old Prussian squirearchy.

Just as the members of the community originally had

equal shares in the soil and equal rights of usage, so they had also an equal share in the legislation, administration, and jurisdiction within the mark. At fixed times and, if necessary, more frequently, they met in the open air to discuss the affairs of the mark and to sit in judgment upon breaches of regulations and disputes concerning the mark. It was, only in miniature, the primitive assembly of the German people, which was, originally, nothing other than a great assembly of the mark. Laws were made, but only in rare cases of necessity. Officials were chosen, their conduct in office examined, but chiefly judicial functions were exercised. The president had only to formulate the questions. The judgment was given by the aggregate of the members present.

The unwritten law of the mark was, in primitive times, pretty much the only public law of those German tribes, which had no kings; the old tribal nobility, which disappeared during the conquest of the Roman Empire, or soon after, easily fitted itself into this primitive constitution, as easily as all other spontaneous growths of the time, just as the Celtic clan-nobility, even as late as the seventeenth century, found its place in the Irish holding of the soil in common. And this unwritten law has struck such deep roots into the whole life of the Germans, that we find traces of it at every step and turn in the historical development of our people. In primitive times, the whole public authority in time of peace was exclusively judicial, and rested in the popular assembly of the hundred, the shire, or of the whole tribe. But this popular tribunal was only the popular tribunal of the mark adapted to cases that did not purely concern the mark, but came within the scope of the public authority. Even when the Frankish kings began to transform the self-governing shires into provinces governed by royal delegates, and thus separated the royal shire-courts from the common mark tribunals, in both the judicial function remained vested in the people. It was only when the old democratic freedom had been long undermined, when military service and tribunals had become a severe burden upon the impoverished free men, that Charlemagne, in his shire-courts, could introduce judgment by Schöffen, lay assesors, appointed by the king's judge,

in the place of judgment by the whole popular assembly.*
But this did not seriously touch the tribunals of the mark.
These, on the contrary, still remained the model even for
the feudal tribunals in the Middle Ages. In these, too, the
feudal lord only formulated the issues, whilst the vassals
themselves found the verdict. The institutions governing a
village during the Middle Ages are but those of an independent village mark, and passed into those of a town as
soon as the village was transformed into a town, i.e., was
fortified with walls and trenches. All later constitutions of
cities have grown out of these original town mark regulations. And, finally, from the assembly of the mark were
copied the arrangements of the numberless free associations of medieval times not based upon common holding
of the land, and especially those of the free guilds. The
rights conferred upon the guild for the exclusive carrying
on of a particular trade were dealt with just as if they were
rights in a common mark. With the same jealousy, often
with precisely the same means in the guilds as in the mark,
care was taken that the share of each member in the common benefits and advantages should be equal, or as nearly
equal as possible.

All this shows the mark organisation to have possessed
an almost wonderful capacity for adaptation to the most
different departments of public life and to the most various
ends. The same qualities it manifested during the progressive development of agriculture and in the struggle of the
peasants with the advance of large landed property. It had
arisen with the settlement of the Germans in Germania
Magna, that is, at a time when the breeding of cattle was
the chief means of livelihood, and when the rudimentary,
half-forgotten agriculture which they had brought with
them from Asia was only just put into practice again. It
held its own all through the Middle Ages in fierce, inces-

---

* Not to be confused with the Schöffen courts after the manner of
Bismarck and Leonhardt, in which lawyers and lay assessors combined
find verdict and judgment. In the old judicial courts there were no lawyers at all, the presiding judge had no vote at all, and the Schöffen
or lay assessors gave the verdict independently. *Engels's footnote.*

sant conflicts with the landholding nobility. But it was still such a necessity that wherever the nobles had appropriated the peasants' land, the villages inhabited by these peasants, now turned into serfs, or at best into *coloni* or dependent tenants, were still organised on the lines of the old mark, in spite of the constantly increasing encroachments of the lords of the manor. Farther on we will give an example of this. It adapted itself to the most different forms of holding the cultivated land, so long as only an uncultivated common was still left, and in like manner to the most different rights of property in the common mark, as soon as this ceased to be the free property of the community. It died out when almost the whole of the peasants' lands, both private and common, were stolen by the nobles and the clergy, with the willing help of the princes. But economically obsolete and incapable of continuing as the prevalent social organisation of agriculture it became only when the great advances in farming of the last hundred years made agriculture a science and led to altogether new systems of carrying it on.

The undermining of the mark organisation began soon after the conquest of the Roman Empire. As representatives of the nation, the Frankish kings took possession of the immense territories belonging to the people as a whole, especially the forests, in order to squander them away as presents to their courtiers, to their generals, to bishops and abbots. Thus they laid the foundation of the great landed estates, later on, of the nobles and the Church. Long before the time of Charlemagne, the Church had a full third of all the land in France, and it is certain that, during the Middle Ages, this proportion held generally for the whole of Catholic Western Europe.

The constant wars, internal and external, whose regular consequences were confiscations of land, ruined a great number of peasants, so that even during the Merovingian dynasty, there were very many free men owning no land. The incessant wars of Charlemagne broke down the mainstay of the free peasantry. Originally every freeholder owed service, and not only had to equip himself, but also to maintain himself under arms for six months. No wonder that even in Charlemagne's time scarcely one man in five could be actually got to serve. Under the chaotic rule of his successors, the freedom of the peasants went still more rapidly to the dogs. On the one hand, the ravages of the Northmen's invasions, the eternal wars between kings, and feuds between nobles, compelled one free peasant after another to seek the protection of some lord. Upon the other hand, the covetousness of these same lords and of the Church hastened this process; by fraud, by promises, threats, violence, they forced more and more peasants and peasants' land under their yoke. In both cases, the peasants' land was added to the lord's manor, and was, at best, only given back for the use of the peasant in return for tribute and service. Thus the peasant, from a free owner of the land, was turned into a tribute-paying, service-rendering appanage of it, into a serf. This was the case in the Western Frankish kingdom, especially west of the Rhine. East of the Rhine, on the other hand, a large number of free peasants, for the most part scattered, occasionally united in villages entirely composed of free men, still held their own. Even here, however, in the tenth, eleventh, and twelfth centuries, the overwhelming power of the nobles and the Church was constantly forcing more and more peasants into serfdom.

When a large landowner—clerical or lay—got hold of a peasant's holding, he acquired with it, at the same time, the rights in the mark that appertained to the holding. The new landlords were thus members of the mark and, within the mark, they were, originally, only regarded as on an equality with the other members of it, whether free or serfs, even if these happened to be their own bondsmen. But soon, in spite of the dogged resistance of the peasants, the lords acquired in many places special privileges in the mark, and were often able to make the whole of it subject to their own rule as lords of the manor. Nevertheless the old organisation of the mark continued, though now it was presided over and encroached upon by the lord of the manor.

How absolutely necessary at that time the constitution of the mark was for agriculture, even on large estates, is shown in the most striking way by the colonisation of Brandenburg and Silesia by Frisian and Saxon settlers, and by settlers from the Netherlands and the Frankish banks of the Rhine. From the twelfth century, the people were settled in villages on the lands of the lords according to German law, i.e., according to the old mark law, so far as it still held on the manors owned by lords. Every man had house and homestead; a share in the village fields, determined after the old method by lot, and of the same size for all; and the right of using the woods and pastures, generally in the woods of the lord of the manor, less frequently in a special mark. These rights were hereditary. The fee simple of the land continued in the lord, to whom the colonists owed certain hereditary tributes and services. But these dues were so moderate that the condition of the peasants was better here than anywhere else in Germany. Hence, they kept quiet when the peasants' war broke out. For this apostasy from their own cause they were sorely chastised.

About the middle of the thirteenth century there was everywhere a decisive change in favour of the peasants. The crusades had prepared the way for it. Many of the lords, when they set out to the East, explicitly set their peasant serfs free. Others were killed or never returned. Hundreds of noble families vanished, whose peasant serfs frequently gained their freedom. Moreover, as the needs of the landlords increased, the command over the payments in kind and services of the peasants became much more important than that over their persons. The serfdom of the earlier Middle Ages, which still had in it much of ancient slavery, gave to the lords rights which lost more and more their value; it gradually vanished, the position of the serfs narrowed itself down to that of simple hereditary tenants. As the method of cultivating the land remained exactly as of old, an increase in the revenues of the lord of the manor was only to be obtained by the breaking up of new ground, the establishing of new villages. But this was only possible by a friendly agreement with the colonists, whether they belonged to the estate or were strangers. Hence, in the documents of this time, we meet with a clear determination and a moderate scale of the peasants' dues, and good treatment of the peasants, especially by the spiritual landlords. And, lastly, the favourable position of the new colonists reacted again on the condition of their neighbours, the bondmen, so that in all the North of Germany these also, whilst they continued their services to the lords of the manor, received their personal freedom. The Slav and Lithuanian-Prussian peasants alone were not freed. But this was not to last.

In the fourteenth and fifteenth centuries the towns rose rapidly, and became rapidly rich. Their artistic handïcraft, their luxurious life, throve and flourished, especially in South Germany and on the Rhine. The profusion of the town patricians aroused the envy of the coarsely fed, coarsely clothed, roughly furnished country lords. But whence to obtain all these fine things? Lying in wait for travelling merchants became more and more dangerous and unprofitable. But to buy them, money was requisite. And that the peasants alone could furnish. Hence, renewed oppression of the peasants, higher tributes, and more corvée; hence renewed and always increasing eagerness to force the free peasants to become bondmen, the bondmen to become serfs, and to turn the common mark land into land belonging to the lord. In this the princes and nobles were helped by the Roman jurists, who, with their application of Roman jurisprudence to German conditions, for the most part not understood by them, knew how to produce endless confusion, but yet that sort of confusion by which the lord always won and the peasant always lost. The spiritual lords helped themselves in a more simple way. They forged documents, by which the rights of the peasants were curtailed and their duties increased. Against these robberies by the landlords, the peasants, from the end of the fifteenth century, frequently rose in isolated insurrections, until, in 1525, the great Peasant War overflowed Swabia, Bavaria, Franconia, extending into Alsace, the Palatinate, the Rheingau, and Thuringia. The peasants succumbed after hard fighting. From that time dates the renewed predominance of serfdom amongst the German peasants generally. In those places where the fight had raged, all remaining rights of the peasants were now shamelessly trodden underfoot, their common land turned into the property of the lord, they themselves into serfs. The North German peasants, being placed in more favourable conditions, had remained quiet; their only reward was that they fell under the same subjection, only more slowly. Serfdom is introduced among the German peasantry from the middle of the sixteenth century in Eastern Prussia, Pomerania, Brandenburg, Silesia, and from the end of that century in Schleswig-Holstein, and henceforth becomes more and more their general condition.

However, this new act of violence had an economic cause as well. From the wars consequent upon the Protestant Reformation, only the German princes had gained greater power. It was now all up with the nobles' favourite trade of highway robbery. If the nobles were not to go to ruin, greater revenues had to be got out of their landed property. But the only way to effect this was to work at least a part of their own estates on their own account, upon the model of the large estates of the princes, and especially of the monasteries. That which had hitherto been the exception now became a necessity. But this new agricultural plan was stopped by the fact that almost everywhere the soil had been given to tribute-paying peasants. As soon as the tributary peasants, whether free men or *coloni*, had been turned into serfs, the noble lords had a free hand. Part of the peasants were, as it is technically known, "evicted" ["gelegt"], i.e., either driven away or degraded to the level of cottars, with mere huts and a bit of garden land, whilst the ground belonging to their homestead was made part and parcel of the demesne of the lord, and was cultivated by the new cottars and such peasants as were still left, in corvée labour. Not only were many peasants thus actually driven away, but the corvée service of those still left was enhanced considerably, and at an ever increasing rate. The capitalistic period announced itself in the country districts as the period of agricultural industry on a large scale, based upon the corvée labour of serfs.

This transformation took place at first rather slowly. But then came the Thirty Years' War. For a whole generation Germany was overrun in all directions by the most licentious soldiery known to history. Everywhere was burning, plundering, rape, and murder. The peasant suffered most where, apart from the great armies, the smaller independent bands, or rather the freebooters, operated uncontrolled, and upon their own account. The devastation and depopulation were beyond all bounds. When peace came Germany lay on the ground helpless, downtrodden, cut to pieces, bleeding; but, one again, the most pitiable, miserable of all was the peasant.

The land-owning noble was now the only lord in the country districts. The princes, who just at that time were reducing to nothing his political rights in the assemblies of Estates, by way of compensation left him a free hand against the peasants. The last power of resistance on the part of the peasants had been broken by the war. Thus the noble was able to arrange all agrarian conditions in the manner most conducive to the restoration of his ruined finances. Not only were the deserted homesteads of the peasants, without further ado, united with the lord's demesne; the eviction of the peasants was carried on wholesale and systematically. The greater the lord of the manor's demesne, the greater, of course, the corvée required from the peasants. The system of "unlimited corvée" was introduced anew. The noble lord was able to command the peasant, his family, his cattle, to labour for him, as often and as long as he pleased. Serfdom was now general; a free peasant was now as rare as a white crow. And in order that the noble lord might be in a position to nip in the bud the very smallest resistance on the part of the peasants, he received from the princes of the land the right of patrimonial jurisdiction, i.e., he was nominated sole judge in all cases of offence and dispute among the peasants, even if the peasant's dispute was with him, the lord himself, so that the lord was judge in his own case! From that time, the stick and the whip ruled the agricultural districts. The German peasant, like the whole of Germany, had reached his lowest point of degradation. The peasant, like the whole of Germany, had become so powerless that all self-help failed him, and deliverance could only come from without.

And it came. With the French Revolution came for Germany also and for the German peasant the dawn of a better day. No sooner had the armies of the Revolution conquered the left bank of the Rhine than all the old rubbish vanished, as at the stroke of an enchanter's wand—corvée service, rent dues of every kind to the lord, together with the noble lord himself. The peasant of the left bank of the Rhine was now lord of his own holding; moreover, in the Code Civil, drawn up at the time of the Revolution and only baffled and botched by Napoleon, he received a code of laws adapted to his new conditions, that he could not only understand, but also carry comfortably in his pocket.

But the peasant on the right bank of the Rhine had still to wait a long time. It is true that in Prussia, after the well-deserved defeat at Jena, some of the most shameful privileges of the nobles were abolished, and the so-called redemption of such peasants' burdens as were still left was made legally possible. But to a great extent and for a long time this was only on paper. In the other German states, still less was done. A second French Revolution, that of 1830, was needed to bring about the "redemption" in Baden and certain other small states bordering upon France. And at the moment when the third French Revolution, in 1848, at last carried Germany along with it, the redemption was far from being completed in Prussia, and in Bavaria had not even begun. After that, it went along more rapidly and unimpeded; the corvée labour of the peasants, who had this time become rebellious on their own account, had lost all value.

And in what did this redemption consist? In this, that the noble lord, on receipt of a certain sum of money or of a piece of land from the peasant, should henceforth recognise the peasant's land, as much or as little as was left to him, as the peasant's property, free of all burdens; though all the land that had at any time belonged to the noble lord was nothing but land stolen from the peasants. Nor was this all. In these arrangements, the government officials charged with carrying them out almost always took the side, naturally, of the lords, with whom they lived and caroused, so that the peasants, even against the letter of the law, were again defrauded right and left.

And thus, thanks to three French revolutions, and to the German one, that has grown out of them, we have once again a free peasantry. But how very inferior is the position of our free peasant of today compared with the free member of the mark of the olden time! His homestead is generally much smaller, and the unpartitioned mark is reduced to a few very small and poor bits of communal forest. But, without the use of the mark, there can be no cattle for the small peasant; without cattle, no manure; without manure, no agriculture. The tax-collector and the officer of the law threatening in the rear of him, whom the peasant of today knows only too well, were people unknown to the old members of the mark. And so was the mortgagee, into whose clutches nowadays one peasant's holding after another falls. And the best of it is that these modern free peasants, whose property is so restricted, and whose wings are so clipped, were created in Germany, where everything happens too late, at a time when scientific agriculture and the newly invented agricultural machinery make cultivation on a small scale a method of production more and more antiquated, less and less capable of yielding a livelihood. As spinning and weaving by machinery replaced the spinning-wheel and the handloom, so these new methods of agricultural production must inevitably replace the cultivation of land in small plots by landed property on a large scale, provided that the time necessary for this be granted.

For already the whole of European agriculture, as carried on at the present time, is threatened by an overpowering rival, *viz.*, the production of corn on a gigantic scale by America. Against this soil, fertile, manured by nature for a long range of years, and to be had for a bagatelle, neither our small peasants, up to their eyes in debt, nor our large landowners, equally deep in debt, can fight. The whole of the European agricultural system is being beaten by American competition. Agriculture, as far as Europe is concerned, will only be possible if carried on upon socialised lines, and for the advantage of society as a whole.

This is the outlook for our peasants. And the restoration of a free peasant class, starved and stunted as it is, has this value—that it has put the peasant in a position, with the aid of his natural comrade, the worker, to help himself, as soon as he once understands *how*.¹

Written by F. Engels in the early half of December 1882

Originally published as an appendix to the German edition of F. Engels's pamphlet *Socialism: Utopian and Scientific,* which appeared in Zürich in 1882

Printed according to the text of the English edition of F. Engels's pamphlet, *Socialism: Utopian and Scientific,* of 1892

---

¹ In the separate printing, released in 1883 under the title, *German Peasant. What Was He? What Is He? What Could He Have Been?,* Engels made the following addition: "But how?—By means of reviving the mark, not in its old, outdated form, but in a rejuvenated form: by rejuvenating common landownership under which the latter would not only provide the small-peasant community with all the prerogatives of big farming and the use of agricultural machinery, but will also give them means to organise, along with agriculture, major industries utilising steam and water power, and to organise them without capitalists by the community itself.

"To organise big farming and utilise agricultural machines means, in other words, to make superfluous the agricultural labour of most small peasants who today work their land themselves. And so that these people, made superfluous in agriculture, would not be left unemployed and would not have to go to towns and cities, it would be necessary to employ them in industry in the village itself, and that can only be profitably organised on a large scale with the aid of steam and water power.

"How to arrange this? Think well on it, German peasants. Only the *Social-Democrats* can help you."—*Ed.*

II

F. ENGELS

ON THE HISTORY OF THE PRUSSIAN PEASANTRY[1]

I consider it necessary to write a few words of explanation about Wolff's present work.

Germany east of the Elbe and north of the Erzgebirge and Riesengebirge constitutes a region re-conquered from the Slavs in the latter half of the Middle Ages, and re-Germanised by German colonists. The conquering German knights and barons who were given this land, acted as village "founders" (Gründer), parcelled up their estates into village lots, each of which was broken up into a number of equal peasant parcels or hides (hufe). Each hide had a homestead and garden in the village itself. The Franconian (Rhine-Franconian and Netherland), Saxon and Frisian colonists drew lots for the hides, in return for which they were required to perform very moderate, strictly specified tributes and services to the founders, i.e., the knights and barons. So long as the peasants fulfilled their services they remained hereditary masters of their hides. Furthermore, they enjoyed the same rights of using the founder's (the subsequent landowner's) woodlands for cutting wood, pasturage, feeding pigs on acorns, etc., as the West-German peasants enjoyed in their communal mark. The village lands were subject to obligatory crop rotation, and were mostly

---

[1] Engels intended this work, written in 1885, as the second part of an introduction to a separate edition of articles by Wilhelm Wolff, titled *The Silesian Billion,* published in Marx's *Neue Rheinische Zeitung* in March and April 1849. A biographical sketch of Wolff, written back in 1876, made up the first part of the introduction. The articles by Wolff, a pupil and associate of Marx and Engels, revealed how the Prussian government, supported by the liberal bourgeoisie, fleeced the peasantry in favour of the Junker landowners under the pretext of redemption of feudal tributes.—*Ed.*

cultivated under the three-course system, being broken up into winter, spring and fallow fields. The fallow and stubble fields served as common pasturage for both the peasant's and the founder's cattle. All village affairs were settled by majority vote at village assemblies of hide owners. The rights of the founder nobles did not go beyond the receipt of tributes and services and the use in common of the fallow and stubble pastures, the appropriation of surplus yields from the woodland, and chairmanship at village assemblies of hide owners, who were all free men. Such, in the main, was the situation of the German peasants settled in the region stretching from the Elbe to East Prussia and Silesia. And it was, on the whole, considerably better than that of the West- and South-German peasants of the same day, who were then already involved in a bitter, constantly renewed struggle with the feudal lords for their former hereditary rights and who had mostly fallen into a much more oppressive dependence, which menaced, and in places even destroyed, their personal freedom.

Needless to say that in the northeast as well, the mounting money requirements of the 14th- and 15th-century feudal lords led to attempts to oppress and exploit the peasants in violation of contracts. But these were by no means on the same scale and as successful as they were in South Germany. The lands east of the Elbe were sparsely populated; the waste lands were still extensive; the cultivation of these waste lands, the extension of cultivation and the founding of taxable villages remained the surest means of enrichment also for the feudal landowner. What was more, relatively big states had arisen along the border of the German Empire and Poland, such as Pomerania, Brandenburg, and the Electorate of Saxony (Silesia was Austrian), and the internal peace therefore was better preserved, and the feuds and highway robberies of the nobles suppressed with a stronger hand than in the dismembered regions along the Rhine, in Franconia and Swabia. But it was the peasant again who suffered most from this perpetual state of war.

It was only in the neighbourhood of conquered Polish and Lithuanian-Prussian villages that the nobles tried ever more frequently to coerce the colonists settled there under the German feudal custom law into the same serfdom as their Polish and Prussian subjects. This was the case in Pomerania and in the Prussian possessions of the Teutonic Order and, to a smaller extent, in Silesia.

Due to their better situation the peasants east of the Elbe remained almost unaffected by the powerful movement of the South- and West-German peasantry in the final quarter of the fifteenth and first quarter of the sixteenth century, and when the revolution broke out in 1525 it produced among them a weak and easily quelled repercussion only in Eastern Prussia. The peasants east of the Elbe left their insurgent brethren in the lurch, and were served their just deserts. In localities where the great Peasant War had raged, the peasants were forthwith turned into serfs subject to arbitrary corvée and burdens, and their free marks were simply turned into the lord's property, where they retained only the usufructs granted by mercy of their master. The same ideal conditions of feudal landownership, for which the German nobility had vainly yearned throughout the Middle Ages, and which it had finally achieved at a time when the feudal economy was disintegrating, were now gradually extended to the lands east of the Elbe. Matters went further than the conversion of the contracted rights of the peasants to the use of the landowner's wood, wherever these had not already previously been curtailed, into usufruct by grace of the landowner, which the latter could at any time withdraw; they went further than unlawful increases in services and tributes. New burdens were imposed, such as relief (a duty payable to the lord by heirs of a deceased peasant landholder), which were regarded as characteristic of serfdom, while the old customary services obtained the nature of services performed only by serfs, and not free men. Thus within less than a hundred years the free peasants east of the Elbe were turned into serfs, first in fact, and then juridically as well.

The feudal nobles, meanwhile, turned more and more bourgeois. They went ever more in debt to the urban capitalist usurer, and money became their most pressing need. Yet money was not to be had from the peasant serfs; only work and farm produce could be squeezed out of them, and the peasant fields, cultivated under most trying conditions, yielded only a minimum surplus above the extremely scanty maintenance of their tillers. Meanwhile, the extensive and profitable abbey land lay alongside, worked by the compulsory labour of dependent peasants and serfs at their owner's account and under expert supervision. The lesser nobles were until then hardly ever able to maintain that type of economy, and the more powerful of them, and the princes, did so in only exceptional cases in their domains. But after the country was pacified it became possible to go in for large-scale farming everywhere, and, on the other hand, such farming was increasingly necessitated by the growing need in money. The cultivation of big estates by means of compulsory serf labour at the lord's account thus gradually provided a source of income to compensate the nobility for the highway robberies that had outlived their time. But where to get the required land? The noblemen, indeed, were owners of bigger or smaller estates, but these were with but a few exceptions parcelled out to hereditary tribute-paying peasants who, provided they produced the stipulated services, had just as much right to their homesteads and hides, and to the village commons, as the gracious lords themselves. A way had to be found; above all, it was necessary to turn the peasants into serfs. For even if the eviction of serfs from house and home was not less illegal and outrageous than that of free tenants, it was nevertheless easier justified by the prevailing Roman law. In a word, after the peasants were propitiously turned into serfs, the required number of them was driven off the soil, or resettled on the lord's land as cottars, or day labourers with hut and garden. The former fortified castle of the noble gave place to his new, more or less open country seat, and, for that very reason, the former free peasant's homestead gave place to a far greater extent to the wretched hut of the serf.

Once the manorial estate—the dominium, as it was known in Silesia—was established, it was only a matter of getting the peasants to cultivate it. And that was where the second advantage of serfdom came to the fore. The former services of peasants fixed by contract, were by no means adequate. In most cases they did not go beyond services for the common weal, such as road- and bridge-building, etc., building work in the manorial castle, and services by women and girls at the manor in various branches of industry and as domestics. But as soon as the peasant was turned serf, and the latter compared by advocates of Roman law to a Roman slave, the gracious lord struck up a new tune. With the acquiescence of the jurists in the courts, he now commanded the peasant to labour for him as much, as often and as long as it suited him. The peasant was obliged to work, cart, plough, sow and harvest for his lord at the first behest, even if his own field went untended and his own harvest perished in the rain. His dues in kind and money were similarly inflated to the utmost.

But that was not all. The no less noble prince of the land —available everywhere east of the Elbe—was also in need of money, much money. In return for letting them subjugate his peasants, the nobles—who were themselves exempt from taxation—allowed him to tax the said peasants. And to top it all, the prince sanctioned the factually prevailing conversion of the lord's former right to preside at the long since suspended free feudal peasant tribunals, into the right of patrimonial jurisdiction and manorial police, whereby the lord of the manor became police chief and, what was more, the sole judge of his peasants, even in cases involving his own person, so that the peasants could complain of the lord only to the lord himself. Thus, he was legislator, magistrate and bailiff *all in one*, and unlimited lord of the manor.

These infamous circumstances, unequalled even in Russia, where the peasants at least had a self-administering community, reached their zenith between the Thirty Years' War and the providential defeat at Jena. The hardships of the Thirty Years' War enabled the nobles to consummate the subjugation of the peasants, and the devastation of countless peasant farmsteads enabled them freely to annex these to their own dominiums. The re-settlement of the population, forced into vagabondage by the ravages of war, offered an excellent pretext for attaching it to the soil as serfs. But that satisfied the nobles only for a short time. The terrible wounds of war were barely healed in the next fifty years, the fields cultivated again, and the population increased, when the landowners felt a new hunger for peasant land and labour. The dominiums were not large enough to consume all the labour that could be knocked out of the serfs—the "knocked out" being used here in its literal sense. The system of turning peasants into cottars, or serf day labourers, had brilliantly justified itself. It gained increasingly in scope in the early eighteenth century, and acquired the name of *eviction of peasants (Bauernlegen)*. As many of the latter were evicted as circumstances permitted; at first a required number was retained for drayage services, and the rest turned into cottars (market-gardeners,[1] cottagers, day labourers, and whatever else they were called), who toiled on the estate year in and year out for a hut and a potato patch and received a miserable day wage in grain, and even less in money. Wherever the gracious lord was rich enough to provide for his own draught animals the spared peasants were also evicted, and their farmsteads annexed to the manorial estate. All the big landed estates of the German nobility, particularly east of the Elbe, are thus pieced together from *stolen peasant holdings*, and should they be taken back from the robbers unrequited, even that would fall short of the latter's just deserts. It is really they who should in addition pay a compensation.

In the course of time the princes of the land realised that this system, ever so profitable to the nobility, was by no means in their interests. The peasants had paid taxes before they were evicted, while their holdings incorporated in the tax-free dominium yielded the state nothing at all, and the newly settled cottars yielded scarcely a farthing. Some of the evicted peasants, superfluous on the estate, were simply driven away, and were thus free, i.e., free and outcast (Vogelfrei). The rural population of the lowlands began to thin out, and ever since the prince had been reinforcing his expensive mercenary host with the much cheaper recruiting among peasants, this was by no means indifferent to him. We therefore find enactment

---

[1] *Dreschgärtner*—literally "thrasher gardeners". This category of serf day labourers was particularly widespread in lower Silesia. In possession of a hut and a plot of gardening land, the market-gardeners performed numerous compulsory services, particularly reaping and thrashing for the lord of the manor.—*Ed.*

upon enactment throughout the eighteenth century which, notably in Prussia, sought to curb the peasant evictions, But they all fared no better than ninety-nine hundredths of all the prodigious waste paper put out by German governments since the capitularies[1] of Charlemagne. They existed only on paper. The nobility paid little heed to them, and the eviction of peasants continued.

Even the terrifying example which the great revolution in France made of the wilful feudal nobility, was terrifying only for a moment. Everything remained as before, and what Frederick II had been unable to do, was even more beyond the reach of his weak and short-sighted nephew, Frederick William III. Then came retribution. On October 14, 1806, the entire Prussian state was smashed in a single day at Jena and Auerstedt, and the Prussian peasant has every reason to celebrate that day, and the day of March 18, 1848, more than all the Prussian victories from Mollwitz to Sedan.[2] It was only then, at long last, that it began to dawn upon the Prussian government, driven back to the Russian border, that the free, landowning sons of French peasants could never be vanquished by sons of serfs daily in fear of banishment from house and home. They realised, at long last, that, so to speak, the peasant also was a human being. The time was ripe for action.

But no sooner was peace made, and the court and government returned to Berlin, than all the good intentions vanished like ice in the March sun. True, the highly-touted edict of October 9, 1807, repealed serfdom and hereditary dependence *in name* (and even that only as of Martinmas of 1810), but in reality it left everything unchanged. Things went no further. The king, as hesitant as he was narrow-minded, was, as always, so much under the sway of the peasant-plundering nobility that four enactments appeared between 1808 and 1810 listing cases

---

[1] *Capitularies*—ordinances of the Frankish kings, so called because they were divided into chapters or sections (Lat. *capitulum*).—*Ed.*

[2] March 18, 1848—the day of the popular uprising in Berlin, which ushered in the 1848 revolution in Prussia.

At Mollwitz (Silesia) Frederick II defeated the Austrians on April 10, 1741, in the War of the Austrian Succession (1740-48).—*Ed.*

in which the gentry could again evict peasants in contradiction to the edict of 1807. Only when Napoleon's war with Russia became imminent, it was recalled that the peasants would be needed again, and an edict was issued on September 14, 1811, which *urged* the peasants and landowners within the space of two years to come to a cordial agreement over a redemption of tributes and services, and of the lord's manorial rights, and stated that a royal commission would eventually enforce such agreements in accordance with special provisions. Its guiding principle was that the peasant became a free owner of the land he retained after he yielded up one-third of his holding (or its worth in money). But even such a settlement, so tremendously advantageous to the nobility, was a mere castle in the air. The nobility temporised in order to gain more, and after two years Napoleon was back in the land.

No sooner was he chased out—to the tune of everlasting promises by the terror-smitten king to grant a constitution and popular representation—than all these splendid promises were again forgotten. On May 29, 1816—scarcely a year after Waterloo!—a declaration was added to the edict of 1811, which sounded quite differently. Redemption of feudal services was no longer the rule but the exception, and affected only such holdings as were entered in the land tax registers (i.e., bigger landed estates) and were already under peasant occupancy in 1749 in Silesia, in 1752 in East Prussia, in 1763 in Brandenburg and Pomerania,* and in 1774 in West Prussia. Certain corvées at sowing and harvesting time were also to be preserved. And when finally in 1817 the redemption commissions were set up in earnest, agrarian legislation moved backward much more rapidly than these commissions moved forward. On June 7, 1821, a fresh ordinance was enacted,

---

* Prussian perfidy knows no bounds. It stands revealed here in bare dates. Why was 1763 taken? Simply because in the following year, July 12, 1764, Frederick II had issued a strict edict which required the recalcitrant nobility under pain of punishment to return to their respective owners within a year the peasant and cottar holdings seized en masse since 1740, and, notably, since the outbreak of the Seven Years' War. Whatever the effect of that edict, in 1816 it was thus brought to nought in favour of the nobility.—*Note by Engels*

whereby the right of redemption was reiterated anew for the larger peasant farmsteads, the so-called "consumer economies", while corvées and other feudal duties were explicitly perpetuated for owners of smaller economies, such as cottars, cottagers and market-gardeners—in brief, for all resettled day labourers. That remained the rule from then on. It was only in 1845 that the redemption of such burdens as well, by means other than mutual agreement of lord and peasant (for which, of course, no law was necessary), was, as an exception, made possible in Saxony[1] and Silesia. Furthermore, the payments for which the services could be redeemed once and for all in terms of money or grain were fixed at 25 times the rent, payable in instalments of not less than 100 thaler, whilst peasants of state domains could, ever since 1809, buy themselves free at a payment of 20 times the rent. In brief the far-famed enlightened agrarian legislation of the "state of reason"[2] had but a single purpose: to save as much of feudalism as could be saved.

The practical result was fully consistent with these wretched ordinances. The agrarian commissions were awake to the benevolent designs of the government, and, as Wolff vividly showed in great detail, saw to it that the peasants were thoroughly fleeced in their redemption settlements with the noblemen. Between 1816 and 1848, 70,582 peasant possessions with a total area of 5,158,827 morgen were redeemed; they represented six-sevenths of all the bonded big peasants. Meanwhile, only 289,651 owners of smaller holdings (including 228,000 in Silesia, Brandenburg and Saxony) redeemed their tributes. The annual total of redeemed service days comprised: 5,978,295 drayage days and 16,869,824 labour days. The gentry was compensated for this, as follows: cash payments—18,544,766 thaler; annual money rents—1,599,992 thaler; annual rents in rye—260,069 scheffels; land given up by

---

[1] Reference is made to the province of Saxony in Prussia.—*Ed.*

[2] *State of reason*—a proverbial state implying the Prussian state. Often used sarcastically. Derives from Hegel's introductory speech to his course of lectures on the history of philosophy at Heidelberg University, October 28, 1816, wherein Hegel claimed that the Prussian state was a state of reason.—*Ed.*

peasants—1,533,050 morgen*. In addition to all the other compensations the former feudal landowners received one third of all former peasant lands.

The year 1848 at last opened the eyes of the callous Junkers, who were as narrow-minded as they were conceited. The peasants—particularly in Silesia, where the latifundian system and its attendant reduction of the population to cottars, was most strongly developed—attacked the castles, burnt the signed redemption papers and forced the gracious lords to renounce in writing all claims to further services. These outrages—infamous also in the eyes of the then ruling bourgeoisie—were, indeed, quelled with armed force and strictly punished. But even the most brainless of Junkers realised that feudal services had become impracticable, and that it was better to receive none than receive them from rebellious peasants. It was a matter of saving what could still be saved, and the landed gentry actually had the audacity of demanding compensations for services that had become impracticable. No sooner was the reaction firmly enough back in the saddle than it granted their wish.

Yet prior to that came the law of October 9, 1848, which suspended all redemption negotiations and their attendant legal proceedings, as well as a number of other lawsuits between landowner and peasant. All the highly lauded agrarian legislation since 1807 was thus doomed. After the so-called National Assembly in Berlin was propitiously broken up and the *coup d'état* turned out successful, the feudal bureaucratic Brandenburg-Manteuffel ministry felt strong enough to strike a hard blow in the interests of the nobility. On December 20, 1848, it issued a provisional ordinance, whereby feudal services were, with only a few exceptions, re-instituted on the old footing, pending further adjustments. It was this ordinance that prompted Wolff to deal with the situation of the Silesian peasants in the *Neue Rheinische Zeitung*.

In the meanwhile, it took more than a year to frame the new and final redemption law of March 2, 1850. The agrarian legislation of 1807-47, which is even now being

---

* See Meitzen, *Der Boden des preussischen Staats,* I, S. 432 ff.

praised to the skies by Prussian patriots, could not have been more strongly condemned than it was, reluctantly enough, in the motives to that law—and it was the Brandenburg-Manteuffel ministry that did it!

Suffice it to say that a few insignificant tributes were simply abolished, others were decreed subject to redemption by conversion into cash rents capitalised at eighteenfold amounts. Rent banks were established as go-betweens for the purpose of collecting the payments; the banks were to pay the landowners twenty times the total of the rent by means of the well-known amortisation operations, while the peasant was freed from all obligations through amortisation payments in the course of 56 years.

In its motives the ministry condemned all previous agrarian legislation, and the commission of the chamber condemned the new law. Its operation was not to extend to the left bank of the Rhine, which had long been liberated by the French Revolution from all that rubbish; the commission concurred with that, because, after all, only one, at the most, of the 109 paragraphs of the bill was applicable there, "whilst all the other decisions are totally unsuited there, and, much rather, would easily cause confusion and needless unrest ... because legislation on the left bank of the Rhine *has gone much further than is presently contemplated* in suspending land services", and it could not be expected of the Rhinelanders to agree to be returned to the new-Prussian ideal conditions.

Feudal forms of labour and exploitation were now at last being tackled in earnest. The redemption of peasants was carried out in several years. The period from 1850 to 1865 inclusively saw the redemption of: 1. the remaining big rural owners, of whom there were only 12,706 with a total land holding of 352,305 morgen; 2. the lesser owners, including cottars. Not quite 290,000 of the latter had bought themselves free before 1848, while no less than 1,014,341 redeemed themselves in the last fifteen years. Accordingly, for the bigger farmsteads the number of redeemed drayage days was only 366,274, and of redeemed labour days, 6,670,507. Similarly, the compensation paid in land was a mere 113,071 morgen, and the annual rent payable in rye was 55,522 scheffels. Furthermore, the gentry received a new annual rent in cash of 3,890,136 thaler, and, besides, a final capital settlement of 19,697,483 thaler.*

The sum which the Prussian landed gentry, including the state domains, had made the peasants pay for the free return of a part of the land that they had earlier—up to this very century, inclusively—stolen from them amounts by Meitzen (Vol. I, p. 437) to 213,861,035 thaler. But that figure is much too small, because a morgen of arable land is therein priced at "*only*" 20 thaler, a morgen of woodland at 10 thaler and a scheffel of rye at 1 thaler, which is much too little. Furthermore, it accounts only for "absolutely authenticated settlements", and thus ignores at least all the privately concluded settlements between the parties concerned. Meitzen himself says that the redeemed burdens cited by him, and, hence, all the compensations paid for them, were only a "minimum".

We may assume, therefore, that the sum paid by the peasants to the nobility and treasury for the redemption of illegally imposed burdens, amounted to at least 300,000,000 thaler, and perhaps a billion marks.

A billion marks, paid to make burden-free only a small portion of the land stolen in the course of the preceding four centuries! It is only a small portion, for a far greater portion was kept by the nobility and treasury in the form of primogenitary and other knightly estates and domains!

Frederick Engels

London, November 24, 1885

First printed as the second part of the introduction to W. Wolff's
Silesian Billion

Published in Zürich in 1886

This is a translation from the German of the text of the Zürich 1886 edition of W. Wolff's book

---

* These figures represent the difference in the totals of Meitzen's two tables (Vol. I, pp. 432 and 434).—*Note by Engels*. (Meitzen's first table cites the totals of redemption operations from 1816 to 1848, and the second cites them from 1816 to 1865 inclusively.)—*Ed*.

III

FROM THE LETTERS
OF KARL MARX AND FREDERICK ENGELS

MARX TO ENGELS

April 16, 1856

... I fully agree with you about the Rhine province.[1] The fatal thing for us is that I see something looming in the future which will smack of "treason to the fatherland". It will depend very much on how things go in Berlin whether or not we are put in the position of the Mayence Clubbists[2] in the old revolution. That would be hard. We who are so enlightened about our worthy brothers on the other side of the Rhine! The whole thing in Germany will depend on the possibility of backing the proletarian revolution by some second edition of the Peasant War. Then matters will go splendidly....

---

[1] Allusion is made to the Rhine province of Prussia.—*Ed.*

[2] The reference is to the German republican democrats of the time of the French bourgeois revolution of 1789-94, who, after the French revolutionary troops captured the fortress of Mayence on October 1792, founded the so-called Mayence Club of the Friends of Equality and Fraternity. The Mayence clubbists called for the abolition of the old feudal order and the establishment of a republican system. They wanted the left bank of the Rhine to secede from Germany and join revolutionary France. Failing to obtain support from the propertied classes—the city merchants and top guildsmen—the Mayence clubbists appealed to the townsmen and the German peasants. But they failed to win support in the countryside because the French occupation, though it destroyed the basic feudal duties, maintained the tax burden and introduced a number of new burdens (military levies, etc.). The indifference of the peasants was one of the main reasons why the Mayence clubbists failed in their purpose. The clubbists went off the scene after Mayence was captured by the Prussians in July 1793.—*Ed.*

MARX TO LASSALLE

April 19, 1859

... I am now coming to *Franz von Sickingen*. To begin with, I must praise the composition and action, and that is more than can be said of any other modern German drama. Secondly, leaving aside the purely critical attitude to this work, it greatly excited me on first reading and will therefore produce this effect to a still greater degree in readers governed more completely by their emotions. This is the second and very important aspect.

Now the other side of the medal: *First*—this is a purely formal matter—since you have written in verse, you might have polished up your iambs with a little more ingenuity. But no matter how *professional poets* may be shocked by such carelessness I consider it on the whole an advantage, since our brood of epigonous poets have nothing left but formal gloss. *Second*: the intended collision is not simply tragic, but is really the tragic collision that spelled the doom, and properly so, of the revolutionary party of 1848-49. I can therefore only most heartily welcome the idea of making it the pivotal point of a modern tragedy. But then I ask myself whether the theme you took is suitable for presenting this collision. Balthasar[1] may really imagine that if Sickingen had raised the banner of opposition to imperial power and open war against the princes instead of concealing his revolt behind a knightly feud, he would have been victorious. But can we subscribe to this illusion? Sickingen (and with him Hutten, more or less) did not go under because of his cunning. He went under because as a *knight* and a *representative of a moribund class* he revolted against that which existed or rather against the new form of what existed. Strip Sickingen of his idiosyncracies and his particular training, natural bents, etc., and what is left is Götz von Berlichingen. Embodied in adequate form in that last-named *pitiable* fellow is the tragic contrast between knighthood, on the one side, and Kaiser and princes, on the other; and that is why Goethe rightly made a hero of him.[2] In so far as Sickingen

---
[1] One of the personages in Lassalle's drama.—*Ed.*
[2] Allusion is made to Goethe's *Götz von Berlichingen.—Ed.*

—and even Hutten himself to a certain extent, although with him, as with all ideologists of a class, such utterances should have been considerably modified—fights against the princes (after all, he takes the field against the Kaiser only because he transformed himself from a kaiser of the knights into a kaiser of the princes), he is really only a Don Quixote, although one historically justified. Beginning the revolt as a knightly feud means nothing else but beginning it in *knightly* fashion. Had he begun it otherwise, he would have had to appeal directly and from the very beginning to the cities and peasants, i.e., precisely to the classes whose development constituted the negation of knighthood.

Therefore, if you did not want to reduce the collision to that presented in *Götz von Berlichingen*—and that was not your plan—then Sickingen and Hutten had to succumb because they imagined they were revolutionaries (the latter cannot be said of Götz) and, just like the *educated* Polish nobility of 1830, made themselves exponents of modern ideas, on the one hand, while on the other they actually represented the interests of a reactionary class. The *noble* representatives of the revolution—behind whose watchwords of unity and liberty there still lurked the dream of the old empire and of club-law—ought not, in that case, to have absorbed all interest, as they do in your play, but the representatives of the peasants (particularly these) and of the revolutionary elements in the cities should have formed a quite important active background. You could then have had the most modern ideas voiced in their most naïve form and to a much greater extent, whereas now, besides *religious* freedom, civil *unity* actually remains the main idea. You would then have had to *Shakespearise* more of your own accord, while I chalk up against you as your gravest fault your *Schillerising*, your transforming of individuals into mere speaking tubes of the spirit of the time. Did you not yourself to a certain extent fall into the diplomatic error, like your Franz von Sickingen, of placing the Lutheran knightly opposition above the plebeian Münzerian opposition?

Further, the characters lack characteristic features. Charles V, Balthasar and Richard of Trier are the exceptions. And yet is there another epoch with more clearly defined characters than the 16th century? To my mind Hutten excessively embodies "inspiration" alone, and that is boring. Was not he at the same time gifted and devilishly witty, and have you not done him a great injustice?

To what extent your Sickingen himself—also, by the way, depicted much too abstractly—is a victim of a collision that did not depend on any of his own designs, is apparent from how he has to preach to his knights friendship with the towns, etc., and how readily he himself, on the other hand applies to the towns the standards of club rule....

ENGELS TO LASSALLE

May 18, 1859

... Now as far as the historical content is concerned, you have depicted with great clarity and justified reference to subsequent developments those two sides of the movement of that time which were of greatest interest to you: the national movement of the nobility, represented by Sickingen, and the humanistic-theoretical movement with its further development in the theological and ecclesiastical sphere, the Reformation. What I like most here is the scene between Sickingen and the Kaiser and that between the legate and the archbishop of Trier. (Here you succeeded in producing a fine specimen of character drawing—a contrast between the aesthetically and classically educated and politically and theoretically far-sighted legate, a man of the world, and the narrow-minded German priest-prince—a portrayal which all the same follows directly from the *representative* nature of the two characters.) The pen picture in the Sickingen-Karl scene is also very striking. In Hutten's autobiography, whose *content* you rightly described as essential, you certainly picked a desperate means of working these facts into the drama. Of great importance is also the talk between Balthasar and Franz in Act V, in which the former expounds to his master the *really revolutionary* policy he should have followed. It is here that the really tragic manifests itself; and it seems to me that just because of the significance that attaches to this fact it should have been emphasised somewhat more strongly already in Act III, where there are several convenient places. But I am again lapsing into minor matters

The position of the cities and the princes of that time is also set forth on several occasions with great clarity and thus the *official* elements, so to speak, of the contemporary movement are fairly well accounted for. But it seems to me that you have not laid due stress upon the non-official, the plebeian and peasant, elements and their concomitant representatives in the field of theory. The peasant movement was in its way just as national and just as much opposed to the princes as was that of the nobility, and the colossal dimensions of the struggle in which it succumbed contrast very strongly with the frivolous way in which the nobility, leaving Sickingen in the lurch, resigned itself to its historical calling, that of lick-spittles. It seems to me, therefore, that also in your conception of the drama which, as you will have seen, is somewhat too abstract, not realistic enough for me, the peasant movement deserved closer attention. While the peasant scene with Joss Fritz is admittedly characteristic and the individuality of this "agitator" is presented very correctly, it does not depict with sufficient force the movement of the peasantry—as opposed to that of the nobility—which already at that time was a swelling torrent. In accordance with *my* view of the drama, which consists in not forgetting the realistic for the idealistic, Shakespeare for Schiller, the inclusion of the sphere of the so superbly variegated plebeian society of that day would have supplied, in addition, quite other material for enlivening the drama, a priceless background for the national movement of the nobility in the foreground, and would have set this movement in the proper light. What wonderfully expressive types were produced by this period of the dissolution of feudal bonds as illustrated by the roaming beggar kings, breadless lansquenets and adventurers of every description—a Fallstaffian background which in an historical drama of *this* kind would have even greater effect than it did in Shakespeare! But apart from this, it seems to me that this relegation of the peasant movement to the rear is precisely the point that erroneously induced you, I believe, to misrepresent also the national movement of the nobility in one respect and at the same time to allow the *really* tragic element in Sickingen's fate to escape you. As I see it, the mass of the nobility directly subject at that time to the Emperor had no intention of concluding an alliance with the peasantry. The dependence of their income on the oppressing of the latter did not permit this. An alliance with the towns would have been more feasible. But no such alliance was effected, or was effected only to a very limited extent. Yet a national revolution of the nobility could have been accomplished only by means of an alliance with the townsmen and the peasants, particularly the latter. Precisely herein lies, in my opinion, the whole tragedy of the thing: that this fundamental condition, the alliance with the peasantry, was impossible, that the policy of the nobility had therefore to be a petty one, that at the very moment when it wanted to assume leadership of the national movement, the *mass* of the nation, the peasants, protested against its leadership and it thus necessarily had to collapse. I am unable to judge to what extent your assumption that Sickingen really did have some connection with the peasants has any basis in history. Anyhow, that is wholly unmaterial. Moreover, as far as I remember, wherever Hutten in his writings addresses the peasants, he just lightly touches on this ticklish question concerning the nobility and seeks to focus the wrath of the peasants on the priests. But I do not in the least dispute your right to depict Sickingen and Hutten as having intended to emancipate the peasants. However, this confronted you at once with the tragic contradiction that both of them were placed between the nobles, who were decidedly *against* this, and the peasants. Here, I daresay, lay the tragic collision between the historically necessary postulate and the practically impossible execution. By ignoring this aspect you reduce the tragic conflict to smaller dimensions, namely, that Sickingen, instead of at once tackling emperor and empire, tackled only a prince (although here too you tactfully bring in the peasants) and you simply let him perish due to the indifference and cowardice of the nobility. Their cowardice would, however, have been motivated quite differently if you had previously brought out more emphatically the rumbling movement of the peasantry and the mood of the nobility, which had become decidedly more conservative on account of the former "Bundschuh" and "Poor Konrad". However, all this is only *one* way in which the peasant and plebeian movement could have been included in the drama. At least ten other ways of doing this just as well or better are conceivable....

ENGELS TO MARX

December 15, 1882

Dear Moor,

Enclosed please find the appendix on the Mark.[1] Be so kind as to send it back on *Sunday*, so that I can revise it on Monday—I was not able to conclude the final revision today.

I consider the view expounded here regarding the condition of the peasantry in the Middle Ages and the rise of a *second* serfdom in the middle of the fifteenth century on the whole incontrovertible. I have gone right through Maurer for all the relevant passages and find nearly all my propositions there, *supported, moreover, by evidence*, while alongside them there is exactly the opposite, but either unsupported by evidence or taken from a period which is *not* that in question. This particularly applies to *Frohnhöfe*, Volume 4, Conclusion.[2] The following contradictions occur in Maurer: 1) his habit of adducing evidence and examples from all periods side by side and jumbled together, 2) the remnants of his legalistic bias, which always gets in his way whenever it is a question of understanding a *development*, 3) the insufficient importance which he attaches to *force* and the part it plays, 4) his "enlightened" prejudice that since the dark Middle Ages steady progress to a better state of things *must* surely have been made; this pre-

---

[1] See p. 135 of this book.—*Ed*.
[2] Engels refers to G. L. Maurer's *History of Manorial Estates and Peasant Farms and the Regulations Governing Them in Germany*, in four volumes. (G. L. Maurer, *Geschichte der Frohnhöfe, der Bauernhöfe und der Hofverfassung in Deutschland*, B. I-IV, Erlangen 1862-63).—*Ed*.

vents him from seeing not only the antagonistic character of real progress, but also the individual retrogressions.

You will find that my product is by no means all of one piece but regular patchwork. The first draft was all of one piece but unfortunately wrong. I mastered the material only by degrees and that is why there is so much patching.

Incidentally, the general re-introduction of serfdom was one of the reasons why no industry could develop in Germany in the seventeenth and eighteenth centuries. In the first place there was the reversed division of labour among the guilds—the *opposite* of that in manufacture: the work was divided *among the guilds* instead of *inside* the workshop. In England at this stage migration to the guildfree countryside took place, but in Germany this was prevented by the transformation of the country people and the inhabitants of the agricultural market towns into serfs. This also caused the collapse of the guilds as soon as the competition of foreign manufacture arose. The other reasons which combined with this in holding back German manufacture I will here omit. . . .

ENGELS TO MARX

December 16, 1882

. . . The point about the almost total disappearance—legal or actual—of serfdom in the thirteenth and fourteenth centuries is the most important to me, because formerly you expressed a divergent opinion on this score. In the East Elbe region the colonisation has established that the *German* peasants were free; Maurer admits that in Schleswig-Holstein at that time "all" the peasants regained their freedom (perhaps somewhat later than the fourteenth century). He also admits that in South Germany this was the period when the bondmen were treated best. More or less the same applies to Lower Saxony (e.g., the new "meiers"[1]

---

[1] Prosperous peasants (in many cases former feudal headmen, or meiers) who were tenants of large holdings, often comprising several

who were in fact hereditary tenants). He is only opposed to Kindlinger's view that serfdom first *arose* in the sixteenth century. But that it was refurbished and appeared in a second edition seems to me indubitable. Meitzen gives the dates at which serfs begin to be mentioned again in East Prussia, Brandenburg, Silesia: the middle of the sixteenth century; Hanssen gives the same data for Schleswig-Holstein. If Maurer calls this a *milder* form of serfdom he is right in comparison with the ninth to eleventh centuries, when the old Germanic slavery still continued, and right too with regard to the legal powers which the lord still had then and later—according to the thirteenth-century law-books—over his serfs. But compared with the *actual* position of the peasants in the thirteenth, the fourteenth and, in North Germany, also the fifteenth centuries, the new serfdom was anything but an improvement. Especially after the Thirty Years' War! It is also significant that while in the Middle Ages the degrees of servitude and serfdom were innumerable, so that the *Sachsenspiegel*[1] gave up speaking of the rights of bondmen, this became remarkably simple after the Thirty Years' War. In brief, I am very anxious to know your opinion....

ENGELS TO MEHRING

July 14, 1893

...I can only repeat about the book what I repeatedly said about the articles when they appeared in *Die Neue Zeit*[2]: it is by far the best presentation in existence of the genesis of the Prussian state. Indeed, I may well say that it is the only good presentation, correctly developing in most matters their interconnections down to the least detail. One

---

holdings of forcibly evicted peasants. The meiers, who were nominally temporary tenants, actually acquired hereditary right to the land.—*Ed.*

[1] *Mirror of Saxony*, a medieval German law-book which expounded local (Saxon) rights by custom.—*Ed.*

[2] Engels refers to F. Mehring's *Legend of Lessing*, a series of articles which appeared in 1892 in *Die Neue Zeit*, theoretical organ of the German Social-Democrats, and in book form in 1893.—*Ed.*

regrets only that you were unable to include the entire further development down to Bismarck and one hopes involuntarily that you will do this at some other time and present a coherent and complete picture from the Elector Frederick William down to old William. You have already made your preliminary investigations and, in the main at least, they are as good as finished. The thing has to be done sometime anyhow before the shaky old shanty comes tumbling down. The dissipation of the monarchical-patriotic legends, while not directly a necessary preliminary for the abolition of the monarchy which screens class domination (inasmuch as a *pure*, bourgeois republic in Germany was outstripped by events before it came into existence), will nevertheless be one of the most effective levers for that purpose.

Then you will have more space and opportunity to depict the local history of Prussia as part of the general misery Germany has gone through. This is the point where I occasionally depart somewhat from your view, especially concerning the preliminary conditions for the dismemberment of Germany and the failure of the bourgeois revolution in Germany during the sixteenth century. When I get down to re-working the historical introduction to my *Peasant War*, which I hope will be next winter, I shall be able to develop there the points in question. Not that I consider those you indicated incorrect, but I put others alongside them and group them somewhat differently.

In studying German history—the story of a continuous state of wretchedness—I have always found that only a comparison with the corresponding French periods produces the right proportions, because what happens there is the direct opposite of what happens in our country. There, we see the establishment of a national state from scattered parts of a feudal state precisely at the time when we go through the period of our greatest decline. There, we see a rare objective logic throughout the course of the process, while we experience more and more dismal dislocation. There, during the Middle Ages, foreign intervention is represented by the English conqueror who intervenes in favour of the Provencal nationality against the Northern French nationality. In a way, the wars with England represent a

Thirty Years' War, which, however, ends in the ejection of the foreign invaders and the subjugation of the South by the North. Then comes the struggle between the central power and vassal Burgundy, supported by its foreign possessions, which plays the part of Brandenburg-Prussia, a struggle which ends, however, in the victory of the central power and conclusively establishes the national state. And precisely at that time the national state completely collapses in our country (in so far as the "German kingdom" within the Holy Roman Empire can be called a national state) and there begins the plundering of German territory on a large scale. This comparison is most humiliating for Germans, but for that very reason the more instructive; yet since our workers have put Germany back again in the forefront of the historical movement it has become somewhat easier for us to swallow the ignominy of the past.

Another especially significant feature of the development of Germany is the fact that neither of the partial states which in the end partitioned Germany between them was purely German—both were colonies on conquered Slav territory: Austria a Bavarian and Brandenburg a Saxon colony—and that they acquired power *within* Germany only by relying upon the support of foreign, non-German possessions: Austria upon that of Hungary (not to mention Bohemia) and Brandenburg that of Prussia. On the western border, the one in greatest jeopardy, nothing of the kind took place; on the northern border it was left to the Danes to protect Germany against the Danes; and in the South there was so little to protect that the frontier guard, the Swiss, even succeeded in tearing themselves loose from Germany!...

ENGELS TO KAUTSKY

May 21, 1895

As for your book,[1] I can say that it gets better the further one reads. Plato and Early Christianity are still inadequately treated, according to the original plan. The medieval

---

[1] Engels refers to Kautsky's *Forerunners of Modern Socialism.—Ed.*

sects are much better treated, and *crescendo*. Best are the Taborites, Münzer, and the Anabaptists. There are very many important economic analyses of political events, paralleled however by commonplaces where there were gaps in research. I have learnt a great deal from the book; it is an indispensable preliminary study for my new revision of the *Peasant War*. There seem to be two important shortcomings:

1. A very inadequate examination of the development and role of the declassed, almost pariah-like, elements wholly outside the feudal structure, who were inevitably bound to come into existence whenever a town was formed; who constituted the lowest stratum of the population of every medieval town and, having no rights, were detached from the *Markgenossenschaft*, from feudal dependence and from the craft guild. This is difficult, but it is the *chief basis*, for by degrees, as the feudal ties were loosened, these elements became the *pre*-proletariat, which in 1789 made the revolution in the suburbs of Paris and which absorbed all the outcasts of feudal and guild society. You speak of proletarians—the expression is ambiguous—and bring in the weavers. You describe their importance quite correctly—but only *after* declassed journeymen-weavers came to exist outside the guilds. Only *in so far as* such existed can you make them your "proletariat". Here there is still much room for improvement.

2. You have not fully grasped Germany's place in the world market, her international economic position, in so far as it is possible to speak of it at the end of the fifteenth century. This position *alone* explains why the bourgeois-plebeian movement, which assumed a religious form, succumbed in England, the Netherlands and Bohemia, and succeeded to a *certain* extent in Germany in the sixteenth century: the success of its *religious disguise*, while the success of the bourgeois content was reserved for the next century and for the countries lying along the new world trade routes which had arisen in the meantime: Holland and England. This is a lengthy subject, which I hope to deal with *in extenso* in the *Peasant War*. If only I were already at it! . . .

IV

FROM THE MANUSCRIPTS OF FREDERICK ENGELS

DECAY OF FEUDALISM AND RISE OF NATIONAL STATES[1]

While the savage battles of the reigning feudal nobility filled the Middle Ages with their clamour, the silent work of the oppressed classes undermined the feudal system throughout Western Europe and created conditions in which ever less room was left for the feudal lord. True, the gentry still carried on as of old in the countryside, tormenting their serfs, leading a life of plenty on their sweat, riding down their crops and raping their wives and daughters. But towns and cities had sprung up all about them: in Italy, in Southern France, and along the Rhine they were the old Roman municipalities risen from their ashes; elsewhere, notably in inner Germany, they were newly founded. Sheltered by walls and moats, they were fortresses more formidable than the strongholds of the nobility, because they could only be taken by a large host. Behind the walls and moats, incorporated in guilds and on a small enough scale, developed the crafts of the Middle Ages. The first capital was being accumulated, and gradually there arose the need in commerce with other towns and with the rest of the world, and with it the means to protect that commerce.

In the fifteenth century the townsmen were already more indispensable to society than the feudal nobility. True, agriculture remained the occupation of the bulk of the people, and, thus, the principal branch of production. But the few free peasants who had here and there survived the encroachments of the nobility, were conclusive proof that in agriculture the main thing lay not in the indolence and

---

[1] The title was affixed by the publishers, since none is given in Engels's manuscript.—*Ed.*

extortions of the nobility, but in the toil of the peasant. Furthermore, the requirements of the nobility itself had also multiplied and changed, so that even for the nobility the towns had become indispensable; were not its only instruments of production, its armour and weapons, obtained in the towns? Domestic fabrics, furnishings and ornaments, Italian silks, Brabantine lace, northern furs, Arabian perfumes, Levantine fruit and Indian spices—everything, barring soap—was bought by the nobility in the towns. A certain world trade had developed; the Italians navigated the Mediterranean and the Atlantic coast up to Flanders, and the Hanseatic towns held sway over the North and Baltic seas against mounting Dutch and English competition. Land communications were maintained between the northern and southern centres of sea traffic; the roads serving them passed across Germany. While the nobility became ever more superfluous and ever more of an impediment to development, the burghers became a class which embodied the further progress of production and commerce, of education, and of social and political institutions.

All these advances made by production and exchange were, indeed, by present-day standards, of a very limited nature. Production was confined exclusively to the guilds, thus retaining its feudal character, and trade to the European seas; it did not extend beyond the Levantine seaports, where Far Eastern products were bartered. But the guilds, petty and limited though they were, and with them the guildsmen, sufficed in reshaping feudal society, and at least continued in motion, while the nobility stagnated.

Furthermore, the burgherdom had *money*—a powerful weapon against feudalism. There was scarcely any room for money in a model feudal farm of the early Middle Ages. The lord obtained all he needed from his serfs, either in the form of labour, or as ready produce; the women spun and wove flax and wool, and produced the clothing; the men tilled the fields; the children tended the lord's cattle and gathered the fruits of the forest, birds' nests and straw; besides, the entire family had still to turn in grain, fruit, eggs, butter, cheese, fowl, young cattle, and countless other things. Every feudal manor was self-sufficient; even military dues were levied in kind; commerce and barter were non-existent, and money was superfluous. Europe had fallen to so low a level, it had begun so completely all over again, that money at the time had less of a social than a purely political function: it was used to *pay taxes*, and was principally obtained by highway *robbery*.

But all that changed. Money again became a common medium of exchange, and its bulk, therefore, multiplied substantially. Even the gentry could no longer do without it, and since they had little or nothing to sell, and since highway robberies had also become far from easy, they were compelled to resort to the urban usurer. Long before the new field-pieces shot breaches into the knightly castle walls, these had already been undermined by money; indeed, gunpowder was, so to say, only an executor in the service of money. Money was the great political leveller in the hands of the burgherdom. Wherever personal relations were superseded by money relations, wherever natural duties gave way to money payments there bourgeois relations took the place of feudal relations. True, the old primitive natural economy in the countryside mostly remained; but entire districts had already appeared where, as in Holland, Belgium and the lower Rhine, the peasants paid their lords money instead of corvées and gavel, where lord and vassal had already made the first and decisive step towards changing into landowner and tenant, and where, consequently, the political institutions of feudalism were losing their social basis in the countryside as well.

The extent to which feudalism was already undermined and inwardly torn by money in the late fifteenth century, is mirrored strikingly by the thirst for gold that reigned at the time in Western Europe. The Portuguese sought *gold* along the African coast, in India and in the entire Far East; *gold* was the magic word that drove the Spanish across the Atlantic Ocean to America; *gold* was the first thing the white man asked about when he set foot on newly discovered soil. This craving for distant voyages and adventures in quest of gold, however much it materialised at first in feudal and semi-feudal forms, was at root already incompatible with feudalism, whose groundwork rested upon agriculture, and whose conquests were essentially directed at *acquiring land*. Moreover, seafaring was a distinctly *bourgeois* occupation, which has left its anti-feudal imprint also upon all the modern navies.

In the fifteenth century feudalism was thus in complete decay throughout Western Europe. Towns with anti-feudal interests, with their own laws and an armed burgherdom, had wedged themselves into feudal regions everywhere, and had made the feudal lords dependent upon them partly socially, through money, and here and there even politically. Even in such localities where particularly favourable conditions had contributed to the progress of agriculture, the old feudal bonds had begun to slacken under the effect of money; only in newly conquered lands, such as Germany's possessions east of the Elbe, or in otherwise backward areas remote from the trade routes, the nobility thrived as of old. Everywhere—in town and village—there were more and more people who above all demanded a stop to the perpetual and senseless wars, to the lordly feuds that perpetuated domestic war even when an alien foe was in the land, and to that state of uninterrupted, senseless devastation that prevailed throughout the Middle Ages. Still too weak to assert their will, these elements found strong support on the topmost rung of the feudal system—royal power itself. And that is where the study of social conditions leads us to conditions of state, and where we pass from economical spheres to politics.

New nationalities gradually developed from the confusion of peoples in the earliest Middle Ages, a process under which the victor is known to have been assimilated by the defeated in most of the former Roman provinces, i.e., the Germanic lord by the peasant and townsman. The modern nationalities are thus also a product of the oppressed classes. How fusion took place here and division there is shown graphically in Menke's map of central Lorraine.* One has only to follow the dividing line between Romance and German names to discover that it coincides, in the main, with the border between the French and German tongues in Belgium and Lower Lorraine as it existed for hundreds of years. There is a narrow disputed zone here and there,

---

* Spruner-Menke, *Hand-Atlas für die Geschichte des Mittelalters und der neueren Zeit*, 3. Aufl., Gotha 1874, Karte No. 32.—*Note by Engels.*

where the two languages fight for precedence; but on the whole it is well established what is German and what Romance. The old Lower Franconian and High German form of most of the names on the map shows, however, that they belong to the ninth, or, at the latest, to the tenth century, and that the border between them was already essentially drawn towards the end of the Carolingian period. On the Romance side, particularly near the language border, there are mixed names composed of a German name and a Romance geographical designation; for instance, west of the Maas near Verdun: Eppone curtis, Rotfridi curtis, Ingolini curtis, Teudegisilo villa, the Ippécourt of today, Récourt la Creux, Amblainecourt sur Aire, Thierville. Those were feudal Franconian countryseats, small German colonies on Romance territory, which sooner or later became Romanised. In the towns, and in some rural localities, there were stronger German colonies which retained their language for a longer period; one such colony, for instance, produced the "Ludwigslied"[1] late in the ninth century; but the oaths of the kings and the nobility in A.D. 842, in which the Romance is already Franconia's official language, prove that most of the Franconian lords were Romanised even earlier.

Once the language groups were bordered off (save the later wars of conquest and extermination, such as were fought with the Elbe Slavs[2]), it was natural that they should serve as a basis for the formation of states and that nationalities began to develop into nations. The rapid collapse of the mixed state of Lorraine shows how vigorously this spontaneous process went on as early as the ninth century. True, all through the Middle Ages the language borders by

---

[1] *Ludwigslied*—a legend of the West-Franconian king, Louis III (of the Carolingian dynasty), and of his victory over the Normans in 881, recorded in the Rhine-Franconian dialect.—*Ed.*

[2] *Elbe Slavs*—a large group of West Slav tribes inhabiting Central Europe between the Elbe and Oder rivers. The Elbe Slavs, who repelled frequent invasions of the German tribes, were attacked at regular intervals by the German feudals after the 10th century. Despite their stubborn resistance, the German feudals conquered their land in a series of sanquinary wars of conquest in the 12th century. The Slav population was partly exterminated and the survivors were turned into serfs and forcibly Germanised.—*Ed.*

no means coincided with state borders, yet every nationality, excluding Italy perhaps, was represented in a specific major European state and the tendency to create national states, which came to the fore ever more clearly and consciously, constitutes one of the most essential levers of progress in the Middle Ages.

In each of these medieval states the king represented the top rung of the whole feudal hierarchy, a supreme head indispensable to the vassals, and yet one against whom they were in a permanent state of rebellion. The principal relationship in feudal economy, that of land tenure by certain personal services and tributes, gave no lack of grounds for controversies even in its original, most simple shape, particularly where so many were interested in finding pretexts for quarrels. How true must this have been, then, for the late Middle Ages, when the relations of tenure in all countries formed a confusing tangle of conceded, withdrawn, renewed, forfeited, altered and otherwise stipulated rights and duties? Charles the Bold, for instance, was the Emperor's feoffee for a part of his lands, and the French king's feoffee for another part; on the other hand, the king of France, his feoffor, was simultaneously the feoffee of Charles the Bold, his own vassal, for certain regions. How could conflicts be avoided? Hence that century-long alternation of the vassals' attraction to the royal centre, which alone could protect them against external foes and against each other, and of their repulsion from that centre, into which that attraction inevitably and perpetually changed; hence that continuous struggle between royalty and vassals, whose tedious uproar drowned out everything else during that lengthy period when robbery was the only source of income worthy of free men; hence that endless, ever renewed succession of treason, assassination, poison, conspiracy and all the other possible abominations which underlay the poetical notion of knighthood and yet were no obstacle to declamation about honour and loyalty.

It is plain that in this general chaos royal power was the progressive element. It represented order in confusion, and the budding nation as opposed to dismemberment into rebellious vassal states. All the revolutionary elements taking shape under the feudalistic surface gravitated just as much towards royalty as the latter gravitated towards them. The alliance of royalty and burgherdom dates back to the tenth century; often interrupted by conflicts, because nothing pursued its course consistently in the Middle Ages, it was each time more firmly and vigorously renewed, until it helped royalty to its final victory, and royalty, by way of reward, subjugated and plundered its ally.

Kings, like burghers, found a mighty support in the rising Estate of *jurists*. With the re-discovery of Roman law there developed a division of labour between the clergy, those legal advisers of feudal times, and the lay jurists. The new jurists were above all an essentially burgher Estate; moreover, the justice they studied, advanced and applied was essentially anti-feudal and, in a certain respect, bourgeois. Roman law is so much the classical juridical expression of the living conditions and collisions in a society exclusively ruled by pure private property that all later legislation was unable to improve on it to any substantial extent. Medieval burgher ownership, however, was still strongly hemmed in by feudal limitations and, for instance, consisted mostly of privileges. Roman law, therefore, was in this far ahead of the bourgeois relations of the time. But all further historical development of bourgeois ownership could only, as was the case, advance towards pure private ownership. This development was bound to spot a mighty lever in Roman law, which contained in ready form everything that the burgherdom of the late Middle Ages still unconsciously sought.

True, in many cases Roman law offered a pretext for greater oppression of the peasants by the nobility. This was so, for instance, whenever peasants could not produce written proof of their freedom from otherwise customary tributes, but this does not alter the case. The nobility would have found such pretexts, and did find them day in and day out, without Roman law. At any rate, it was an enormous advance that a law was enforced which contained no inkling of feudal relations and fully anticipated modern private ownership.

We have seen how the feudal nobility became economically superfluous, and even obstructive, in late medieval society, and how, even politically, it stood in the way of urban development and the development of national states, which were then only possible in the form of monarchies. But for all that it had been sustained by its monopoly in warcraft; no wars could be waged, no battles fought, without it. This, too, was to change. The final step was to be made to show the feudal nobles that the period of their social and political domination had come to an end, that they were no longer needed in their capacity of knights, not even in the battlefield.

To fight the feudal system with a feudal army in which the soldiers were bound more closely to their direct suzerains than to the royal army command, was obviously to move in a vicious circle and not come off the spot. Ever since the early fourteenth century the kings strove to do away with such feudal hosts and to create their own armies. The proportion of recruited troops and mercenaries in the royal armies grew steadily from then on. At first they were mostly foot-soldiers, the scum of the towns and escaped serfs, Lombards, Genoese, Germans, Belgians, etc., employed in capturing towns and for garrison duty, and at first scarcely useful in open battle. But late in the Middle Ages we also find horsemen who go into the pay of alien princes with their who-knows-how-assembled followings and thereby spell the inevitable doom of feudal warcraft.

At the same time the basic condition for a war-worthy infantry took shape in the towns and among free peasants wherever such were available or had newly appeared. Until then the knights with their mounted retinue were not just the kernel, but the army itself; the accompanying mob of serf foot-soldiers did not count and seemed to be on hand in the open field simply for the purposes of flight or plunder. As long as feudalism was in its zenith until the end of the thirteenth century it was the cavalry that fought and decided all battles. But from then on things change and, indeed, simultaneously in various places. The gradual disappearance of serfdom in England created a numerous class of free peasants, yeomen or tenants, who provided the raw material for a new infantry conversant in the use of bow and arrow, the English national weapon of that day. The introduction of archers, who always fought on foot, whether or not mounted on the march, caused a marked change in the tactics of the English army. From the fourteenth century the English knights preferred to fight on foot wherever the terrain and other conditions were suitable. Behind the archers, who opened battle and wrought confusion in enemy ranks, a compact phalanx of dismounted knights waited for the enemy attack or for a suitable moment to attack themselves, while only a part of them remained on horseback to render support with flank assaults. The succession of English victories in France at that time reposed principally on this revival of the defensive element in the army; and are mostly just as much defensive battles with an offensive impact as were those of Wellington in Spain and Belgium. After the French adopted new tactics—possibly after mercenary Italian crossbowmen filled the place of the English bowmen in their host—the English victories ceased.

Similarly, early in the fourteenth century the infantry of the Flandrian towns ventured—and often with success —to oppose the French knights in open battle, and Emperor Albrecht's attempt to betray the free (reichsfreie) Swiss peasants to the Archduke of Austria, that is, to himself, gave impetus to the formation of the first modern infantry of European fame. In the victories of the Swiss over the Austrians, and notably over the Burgundians, armoured knights—mounted or otherwise—suffered the final setback at the hands of foot-soldiers, the feudal host at the hands of a budding modern army, knights at the hands of townsmen and free peasants. And the Swiss, in confirmation of the bourgeois nature of their first independent republic in Europe, instantly *turned* their war fame *into silver*. All their political considerations evaporated; the cantons turned into recruitment centres soliciting mercenaries for the highest bidder. Elsewhere, too, and particularly in Germany, the drums beat lustily for recruits, but the cynicism of a government, whose sole purpose appeared to be the sale of its countrymen, remained unmatched until the German princes surpassed it in the days of the deepest national degradation.

Then, also in the fourteenth century, gunpowder and artillery were introduced to Europe through Spain by the Arabs. Until the end of the Middle Ages firearms remained unimportant, and conceivably so, because the bows of the English bowmen at Crecy shot just as far and possibly surer—though, perhaps, with less effect—than the smooth-bored guns of the infantrymen at Waterloo. The field-piece was also still in its infancy; the heavy guns, meanwhile, had repeatedly knocked breaches into the walls of knightly castles and forecast to the feudal nobility that gunpowder sealed the fate of its reign.

The spread of the art of printing, the revived study of antique literature, the entire cultural movement, which gained strength and became ever more universal since 1450—all this was propitious to the burgherdom and to royalty in their fight against feudalism.

The cumulative effect of all these causes, which increased from year to year through their mounting action upon each other that drove them increasingly in the same direction, secured the victory over feudalism in the latter half of the fifteenth century if not as yet for the burgherdom, then for monarchy. Everywhere in Europe, including the outlying regions that had not yet gone completely through the stage of feudalism, royal power all at once obtained the upper hand. On the Iberian Peninsula two local Romance groups combined in a Spanish kingdom and the Provencal tongue of the Aragon state was overpowered by the Castilian literary tongue; the third group unified its language area, excluding Galicia, into the kingdom of Portugal, the Iberian Holland, turned its back upon the hinterland, and affirmed its right to a separate existence through its maritime activities.

In France Louis XI succeeded at last, after the fall of the Burgundian buffer state,[1] in establishing national unity personified in royal power, over an as yet limited area to an extent that his successor was able to interfere in Italian affairs, and this unity was only once briefly jeopardised by the Reformation.[2]

---

[1] *The Duchy of Burgundy*—broke up after the death of Charles the Bold in 1477; a large part of the Burgundian possessions became part of the kingdom of France, and the rest (the Netherlands, etc.) fell into the hands of the Hapsburgs.—*Ed.*

[2] Engels refers to the movement of Huguenots, the French Calvinists, who advocated a religious reformation. The movement was suppressed in the so-called Huguenot (religious) Wars (1562-94).—*Ed.*

England had at last given up its quixotic wars of conquest in France, which would have bled it white in the long run; its feudal nobility sought to make up for them in its Wars of the Roses, and got more than it bargained for. It exterminated itself and brought the house of Tudor to the throne, whose power surpassed that of all its predecessors and successors. The Scandinavian countries were long since unified, Poland, with its as yet unweakened monarchy, approached its zenith after unification with Lithuania, and even in Russia the overthrow of the appanaged princes and the liberation from the Tatar yoke went hand in hand and were finally sealed by Ivan III. In all Europe there were only two countries—Italy and Germany—where royalty and the national unity that was then impossible without it, either did not exist at all, or existed on paper only.

AD "PEASANT WAR"[1]

The Reformation—Lutheran and Calvinist—is the No. 1 bourgeois revolution, the peasant war being its critical episode. The decay of feudalism and the development of towns are two [processes][2] furthering decentralisation, whence the direct requirement of absolute monarchy as a power that would cement nationalities. It *had to be* absolute because of the centrifugal nature of all the elements. But its absolutist nature must not be taken in its vulgar sense; [it developed] in constant struggle with either the representatives of Estates, or the rebellious feudal lords and towns; it did not abolish Estates anywhere; thus, it should rather be designated as an *estate* monarchy (still feudal, in decay, and bourgeois in embryo).

Revolution No. 1—which was more European than English and spread in Europe much more rapidly than the

---

[1] Written by Engels when he wanted to revise his *Peasant War in Germany* and evidently a fragment of the plan for an introduction or introductory section of the revised edition. The notes are on a separate sheet of paper. This ms was first published in 1948 in the "Marx and Engels Archives", Vol. X, in Russian.—*Ed.*

[2] The text in brackets is given by the publishers.—*Ed.*

French—triumphed in Switzerland, Holland, Scotland, England, and, to a certain extent, in Sweden (under Gustavus Vasa) and Denmark—here in its orthodox-absolutist form only in 1660.

I.[1] Causes in Germany. German history from its beginning. The end of Germany after the heroic days of the migration of nations. Only re-established through France by Charlemagne. Therewith the idea of a Roman Empire. Revived through Otto. More non-German than German. Germany's ruin due to such policy—the robbery of Italian towns—under the Hohenstaufens. This intensifies disunity, *excepto casu revolutionis* (to say nothing of uprisings). Development of the Great Interregnum[2] until the fifteenth century. Rise of the towns. Decay of the feudal system, which had at no time reached its zenith in Germany, under the pressure of the princes (the Emperor as sovereign *against*, and as Emperor, *for* the imperial knights). Gradual liberation of peasants, until the reaction in the fifteenth century. Materially, Germany is quite abreast of the countries of that day. Decisive that Germany, provincially disunited and *long spared from invasions*, did not experience so strong a need in national unity as France (Hundred Years' War), Spain, just re-conquered from the Moors, Russia, that had only then driven out the Tatars, and England (Wars of the Roses), and also that the Kaiser's authority was so wretched at the time.

II. The Renaissance in its European variety, based on the general collapse of feudalism and the rise of the towns. Then [the appearance] of absolutist national monarchies everywhere save Germany and Italy.

III. The nature of the Reformation as the only possible *popular* expression of universal aspirations, etc.

---

[1] The text designated by Engels in the ms under I, follows the text under II.—*Ed.*

[2] *Great Interregnum*—the period of twenty years which followed the termination of the Hohenstaufen dynasty (1254) and lasted until 1273; period of struggle for the imperial crown between various pretenders, marked by ceaseless conflicts and discord among the princes, knights and towns.—*Ed.*

NOTES ON GERMANY

1. INTRODUCTION, 1500-1789

1. Germany is more and more disunited and its centre weakened towards the end of the fifteenth century, while France and England are more or less centralised and their nations are taking shape. That is impossible in Germany because, firstly, feudalism developed there later than in the countries that suffered conquest[1]; secondly, Germany had French and Slav composite parts, and regarded Italy as its own, and Rome as its centre—hence, no *national* complex; thirdly, and this is most important, because the provinces and groups of provinces were still completely isolated from one another, there were no communications, etc., (cf. Peasant War); the Hansa, the Rhine League and the Swabian League[2] represented natural but dissociated groups.

Ad I. Spain, France, England take shape as constitutionally national states towards the close of the fifteenth century. This consolidation is epoch-making for the fifteenth century. (Spain—a fusion of the Catalan and Castilian nations. Portugal, the Iberian Holland, won its right to a separate existence by its seafaring, France by dynastic power, which gradually absorbed the entire nation. England—by the Wars of the Roses, which exterminated the aristocracy. In England only after it had to give up its quixotic plans of conquest in France—much like the German campaigns against Rome—which would have bled her white, like Germany was bled white by hers). Germany would have been centralised in spite of its economic disjunction and even earlier (under the Ottos, for example) if it had not been for 1) the title of Roman Emperor with its pretensions to world domination, which ruled out the constitution of a national state, and squandered strength in the

---

[1] Allusion is made to the countries of Western Europe, which were part of the Roman Empire and were conquered by German tribes in the 4th-5th centuries.—*Ed*.

[2] The Swabian and Rhine leagues of South- and West-German towns were framed in the seventies of the 14th century with the purpose of guarding trade routes and repelling the attacks of feudal lords. Late in the 14th century these loosely-knit town leagues fell apart.—*Ed*.

Italian campaigns of conquest (whose effects were felt in Austria until 1866!), in which German interests were constantly betrayed, and 2) the independent elective empire, which precluded the embodiment of the nation in an imperial dynasty, and, instead, always, and particularly in the decisive fifteenth century, changed dynasties as soon as the power became too great for the liking of the princes. In France and Spain there also was economic disjunction, overcome by force.

The "Kulturkampf" between Emperor and Pope[1] in the Middle Ages dismembered both Germany and Italy (where the Pope obstructed national unity and, at the same time, often seemingly championed it, but in a way that Dante, for instance, saw Italy's saviour in a foreign emperor) and in 1500 the Pope had already laid himself across Italy as a medium prince and made unity physically impossible.

2. Yet Germany would have consolidated through the natural development of commerce and the Germanisation of the Slavs [along the Elbe], and the loss of the French provinces[2] and Italy, because the world trade route lay across Germany—if it had not been for two decisive events:

1) The German burgherdom made its revolution—which, in the spirit of the times, had a religious form, that of the Reformation. But how wretchedly! It was not to be done without the imperial knights and the peasantry; but all three Estates were impeded by their conflicting interests: the knights were oppressors of peasants and often robbers of towns (cf. Mangold von Eberstein), which were likewise skinners of the peasantry (cf. the Ulm Council and the Peasants). The imperial knights were the first to rise, but were left in the lurch by the burghers, and failed; the peasants rose, and were *directly fought* by the burghers. Simultaneously, the bourgeois religious revolution was emasculated to such an extent that it even suited the *princes*, who took

---

[1] In ironically calling the struggle of the medieval German Emperors with the Popes a "Kulturkampf", Engels hints at Bismarck's conflict with the Pope and the Catholic Party of the Centre in 1872-79, which has gone down in history under that name.—*Ed.*

[2] Allusion is made to Franche-Comté and French Lorraine, which originally were part of the medieval German Empire, and were subsequently turned over to France.—*Ed.*

leadership into their own hands. The specific theologico-theoretical nature of the German sixteenth-century revolution. Preponderant interest in things that are not of this world. Abstraction from miserable reality is a basis for the latter-day theoretical superiority of the Germans, from Leibnitz to Hegel.

2) The world trade route withdraws from Germany, driving Germany into an isolated corner; the power of the burghers is thus broken, as well as that of the Reformation.

3. The result is that, along the principle of *cuius regio, eius religio*,[1] Germany actually breaks up into a predominantly Protestant north, a predominantly Catholic but strongly mixed southwest, and an exclusively Catholic southeast. Herein the seeds of the defective development in 1740-1870. (Prussia, the split between North and South and, finally, Small Germany and Austria.) An opposite process in France. Suppression of the Huguenots (see *Notes*, p. 2[2]).

3. Once condemned to passivity and retrogression in industry, Germany was bound to be more exposed to the influences of political exigencies than industrially active and progressive countries (elaborate upon this in general). The split into two parties makes civil war the order of the day. Enumeration of wars up to 1648—a civil war. The French take advantage of the situation and enter into alliance with, and *pay, the Protestant princes and German mercenaries*. This culminates in the Thirty Years' War (the Irish in Germany during the Thirty Years' War, and the Germans in Ireland in 1693 and 1806[3]). An account of the destruction. Economical, social and political results: concessions to France; Denmark and Sweden gain a foothold in Germany; the right of the guaranteeing powers to interfere; total collapse of the central authority; *Europe guarantees* to the German princes the right of insurrection against the Emperor, civil war and high treason.

---

[1] *Cuius regio, eius religio,* the Latin for "whose reign, his also the religion", which principle served as basis for the religious peace of Augsburg of 1555 (see footnote to p. 50).—*Ed.*

[2] See the fragment of the second manuscript of "Notes on Germany", p. 196 in this book.—*Ed.*

[3] Engels alludes to the German mercenaries employed by the English in policing Ireland and suppressing the Irish national liberation movement.—*Ed.*

4. 1648-1789.

a. *Political circumstances.* The German princes exploit the Westphalian peace and compete in selling themselves to foreign masters. France takes advantage of German weakness to seize all Germany's French possessions and to round out Alsace. France's historical rights and the Teutonic cry of "thieves"[1]. The language border remains unchanged (see Menke[2]) since about A.D. 1000, save the districts left of the Vosges. This in general. In particular: the rise of a power—Prussia—in the north, competing with Austria and the Empire. The division into North and South begins to materialise. A critique of Prussian history. Frederick II. The rise of Russia and the submission of Frederick II to Russian policy. Civil wars are now wars of competition between Austria and Prussia.

b. *Economical.* For all that, *slow recovery from the effects of the Thirty Years' War* and the slow re-ascension of the burgherdom. It was only its *infamous* capacities that made this ascent possible in such circumstances. For all that, economic progress was made possible only by political intervention—infamy of the princes and the money paid to them from abroad. This proves how low Germany had fallen economically. This period sees the inception of the patriarchal regime. After 1648 the state begins to perform social functions, compelled to do so by financial difficulties. Wherever this was not done there was stagnation (the Westphalian bishoprics). What degradation! And how wretched the help of the state! Totally passive in relation to the world market. Able to gain something from the big world wars (the American and the revolutionary wars up to 1801) only in the capacity of *neutrals.* On the other hand, helpless in the face of robber states. (This shameful situation in Europe was eliminated by the French Revolution.)

---

[1] The reference is to the claims made by German chauvinists to Alsace and Lorraine on the pretext of "historical" rights of the medieval German Empire. Marx and Engels always emphasised that the historical destinies of Alsace and Lorraine have been linked with France since the French bourgeois revolution of 1789-94 and condemned Bismarck's government for annexing them in 1871.—*Ed.*

[2] Spruner-Menke, *Hand-Atlas für die Geschichte des Mittelalters und der neueren Zeit,* 3. Aufl. Gotha 1874, Karte No. 32.—*Ed.*

c. Literature and language have declined. The petrified dogmatism of theology. Degeneration of other sciences in Germany. Yet there are rays of hope; J. Böhme (again a harbinger of the coming philosophers), Kepler, Leibnitz—once again abstraction from reality. *Bach*.

d. The situation in Germany in 1789. a) Agriculture—the situation of the peasants. Serfdom, corporal punishment, tributes. b) Industry—starving and miserable; essentially manual labour. In England—the beginning of modern industry, while German industry is doomed before it has fully developed. c) Trade—passive. d) The social position of the burghers in relation to the nobility and the government. e) Political obstacles to progress: disunity. Account by Menke. Customs barriers, impediments to inland navigation. Free trade choked at inner borders through dismemberment. Customs duties are mostly urban consumer taxes.

The princes are incapable of doing good, even when enlightened, as were the patrons of Schubart[1] and Karl-August; all of them ready to join the Rhine League rather than risk a war. The 1806 invasion was a test that could have cost them their lives. Each of these 1,000 princes is an absolute monarch. They are uncouth, uneducated ruffians who could not be expected to co-operate. Whims always in plenty (Schlözer). Traffic in recruits for the American War. Their *very existence* was their biggest offence. Along the eastern border Prussia in the North and Austria in the South stretch grasping hands for territory; they are the only two that could have mended matters if there had been only one of them. But the inevitable competition of the two made every expediency impossible. A real dead-end. Help could come only from outside. It came from the French Revolution. Only two signs of life: the military capacity, on the one hand, literature, philosophy and conscientious, objective scientific research, on the other. While in France there is a preponderance of first-class political writers as early as the eighteenth century, in Germany everything boils down to escaping from reality to idealistic

---

[1] Engels refers to the German princes (Duke Leopold of Dassau and Duke Ernst-Frederick of Coburg, etc.) who patronised the 18th century German agronomist, Schubart, and applied his farming methods on their estates.—*Ed.*

spheres. "*The Man*" and the development of the language; in 1700 barbarism, in 1750 Lessing and Kant, then Goethe, Schiller, Wieland, Herder; Gluck, Händel, Mozart.

1789-1815

1. The German enclaves in Alsace-Lorraine,[1] etc., half under French sway, join the French Revolution; this offers a pretext for war. Prussia and Austria are now *suddenly single-minded*. Valmy. Defeat of line formation tactics by massed artillery. Fleurus and Jemappes. Failure of the Austrian cordon tactics?[2] Seizure of the left bank of the Rhine. Rejoicing of peasants and free-minded towns, which not even the separate extortions and Napoleon's blood tax could dispell. The Peace of Amiens and the imperial deputation. The principal result: abolition of the Empire. The Rhine League.[3] Napoleon sweeps out the small states, but, unfortunately, far too little. He is always revolutionary as opposed to the princes. He would have gone further if the lesser princes had not prostrated themselves so abjectly at

---

[1] The reference is to the possessions of German imperial princes (mainly clerical) in Alsace and Lorraine. After these provinces were annexed to France the princes became vassals simultaneously of the French King and the German Emperor. The French bourgeois revolution, which spread to Alsace and Lorraine and secularised all church lands, caused a conflict between the princes and the French government. The appeal of the princes to the Empire was one of the pretexts for intervention by the reactionary German states in the domestic affairs of France.—*Ed.*

[2] On September 20, 1792, at Valmy the French revolutionary army defeated the Prussian troops of the Duke of Braunschweig. On November 6, 1792, the French routed an Austrian army at Jemappes in Belgium. On June 26, 1794, at Fleurus, near Charleroi, they defeated an Austrian army under the Duke of Coburg.—*Ed.*

[3] On concluding a short-lived peace with Austria (1801 at Luneville) and England (March 1802 at Amiens), Napoleon distributed the small possessions of the clerical imperial princes and "free towns" among his German vassals—the bigger lay princes, who convened a special "imperial deputation" in 1803. The final blow to the medieval German Empire was dealt by Napoleon in 1806, when—after resuming the war against Austria and defeating it again—he formed the Rhine League of 16 German states that had officially broken away from the Empire. The imperial title and imperial institutions were soon abolished and the Hapsburg dynasty had to content itself with the title of Austrian Emperors.—*Ed.*

his feet. Napoleon's mistake in 1806 was that he did not crush Prussia to the end. Germany's economic situation during the continental blockade. This period of the greatest abasement from abroad coincides with a brilliant period in literature and philosophy, and the acme of music in Beethoven.

FROM THE SECOND MANUSCRIPT OF "NOTES ON GERMANY"[1]

During the *Huguenot Wars* respect for the kingdom, as representative of the nation, was already so great that foreign alliances and military compacts were taken seriously and recognised by public opinion *only* if they were concluded with the king. All others were always viewed as rebels or traitors. This was never more plain than after the death of Henry III, when Henry IV achieved final victory only by dint of his royal name.

The eventual suppression of Protestantism in France is no loss to France, as testified by Bayle, Voltaire and Diderot. Similarly, even if such suppression would not have been a misfortune to Germany, it would have been one *to the world at large*. It would have forced the Catholic *form* of development of the Romance countries upon Germany, and since the English form of development was also half Catholic and half medieval (universities, etc., colleges, public schools, are all Protestant monasteries) the entire German Protestant educational system (education at home or at private pensions, free-living students electing their own collegiate board) would have vanished and European intellectual development would have become too homogeneous. France and England have exploded the prejudices of the *matter*, and Germany of the *form*, or *pattern*. Hence, partly, the shapelessness of everything German, producing great shortcomings to this very day, such as the system of small states, but it was of tremendous benefit to the nation's ca-

---

[1] The second and third manuscripts, which comprise separate fragments under the general title of *Notes on Germany. 1789-1873*, were published along with the first manuscript in the "Marx and Engels Archives", Vol. X. Only one fragment, to which Engels refers in his first manuscript, is given in this book.—*Ed.*

pacity of developing that will bear full fruit only in the future, once this one-sided phase itself will be overcome.

Moreover: *German Protestantism is the only modern form of Christianity worthy of criticism.* Catholicism was *beneath all criticism* already in the eighteenth century, and an object of *polemics* (what asses those Old-Catholics![1]). English Protestantism broke up into dozens of sects without theological development, or with one whose every stage was marked by the appearance of a sect. The German alone has a theology and, thus, an object of criticism—historical, philological and philosophical. *This was produced by Germany* and, though absolutely essential, impossible without German Protestantism. A religion like the Christian cannot be destroyed by ridicule and invective *alone*, it has also to be *overpowered scientifically*, i.e., *historically explained*, and this not even the natural sciences can manage.

---

[1] *Old-Catholics*—a group of German Catholics who in 1871 protested against the dogma of papal infallibility and favoured a moderate reform of the Catholic Church.—*Ed.*

NAME INDEX

A

Alba, Fernando Alvarez de Toledo (1507-1582)—Spanish vicegerent in the Netherlands; cruelly suppressed popular uprising during Dutch bourgeois revolution of late 16th century—85.

Albrecht I (1250-1308)—Austrian Archduke; from 1298 German Emperor—186.

Albrecht III (1443-1500)—Duke of Saxony; headed punitive expedition against popular uprising in the Netherlands in 1491-1492, and Frisian peasant insurrection in 1497 —66.

Anton (1489-1544)—Duke of Lorraine (1508-1544); in 1525 organised bloody reprisals against rebel peasantry of Alsace; an opponent of the Reformation—120, 122.

Arnold von Brescia (c. 1100-1155)—medieval Italian reformer, ideologist of movement of townsmen against the Pope and other clerical feudal lords in Rome and other towns; executed as a heretic—43, 44.

Aylva, Syaard—leader of Frisian peasant insurrection in 1497—66.

B

Bach, Johann Sebastian (1685-1750)—great German composer—194.

Bach, Walter — lansquenet, joined uprising of South-German peasants in 1525; one of leaders of Allgäu troop; betrayed peasants in the decisive moment and escaped to Switzerland—111, 113.

Baden, Margrave of—see Philip I.

Bakunin, Mikhail Alexandrovich (1814-1876)—Russian revolutionary and publicist, participated in the 1848-1849 revolution in Germany; Narodnik and an ideologist of anarchism, sworn enemy of Marxism in the First International; was expelled from International at Hague Congress (1872) for dissidence—22.

Ball, John—English country parson; popular preacher, called for overthrow of feudal lords and for ancient Christian equality and common ownership; one of inspirers of peasant uprising in England in 1381; after defeat of uprising was quartered (1381)—43, 45.

Bamberg, Bishop of—see Weigand.

Bantelhans—one of leaders of "Poor Konrad" and the peasant uprising in Württemberg and mountain regions of Swabia in 1514—73.

Barnabás—Hungarian priest, active participant in peasant war of 1514 in Hungary—77.

Báthory, István (died in 1535)—member of a prominent feudal family in Transylvania; headed an army sent to suppress peasant uprising in Hungary under Georg Dózsa in 1514—76.

Bayle, Pierre (1647-1706)—French philosopher, sceptic, critic of religious dogmatism—196.

Beethoven, Ludwig van (1770-1827)—great German composer—196.

Berlichingen, Götz von (1480-1562)—German knight, sought to utilise peasant uprising of 1525 for personal gain; elected to head "Gay Bright Troop", betrayed peasants in the decisive moment—93, 94, 95, 96, 105, 106, 167, 168.

Berlin, Hans—town councillor of Heilbronn; after the town was taken by insurgent peasants in 1525 tried to induce them to adopt a more moderate programme—95, 104.

Bismarck, Otto von (1815—1898)—First Chancellor of German Empire (1871-1890), representative of Prussian Junkerdom; unified Germany by reactionary means; introduced Anti-Socialist Law (1878-1890)—143, 175.

Boccaccio, Giovanni (1313-1375)—eminent Italian man of letters, poet of the Renaissance—44.

Böheim, Hans (Hans the Piper)—shepherd and popular preacher at Niklashausen, inspirer of peasant movement in bishopric of Würzburg and its vicinity; burnt at the stake in 1476—63, 64, 65.

Böhme, Jakob (1575-1624)—German artisan, mystic philosopher; voiced a number of notions on the dialectical development of the world—194.

Bonaparte, Louis—see Napoleon III.

Brandenburg-Ansbach, Margrave of—see Casimir.

Brandenburg, Friedrich Wilhelm, Count of (1792-1850)—Prussian general; headed reactionary ministry in Prussia in 1848-1850—163.

Bright, John (1811-1889)—English Liberal, advocate of Free Trade; together with Cobden headed the Anti-Corn Law League—12.

Burgbernheim, Gregor von—one of leaders of peasant insurrection in Principality of Ansbach in 1525—108.

C

Caesar, Gaius Julius (c. 100-44 B. C.)—distinguished Roman general and statesman—137.

Carolingians—dynasty of Frankish kings (8th-9th centuries)—182.

Casimir (1481-1527)—Margrave of Brandenburg-Ansbach, offspring of Franconian Branch of Hohenzollerns; organised reprisals against insurgent Ansbach and Rothenburg peasants and townsmen—105, 107-11.

Charlemagne (742-814)—King of the Franks (768-814), from 800 emperor—143, 145, 160, 189.

Charles the Bold (1433-1477)—

Duke of Burgundy; headed struggle of major French feudal lords against Louis XI; in 1477 was routed by the Swiss in the Battle of Nancy—183.

Charles V, Habsburg (1500-1558) —King of Spain (1516-1556) and German Emperor (1519-1556)—168.

Csáky, Nikolaus—Bisnop of Csanád; killed by peasant insurgents in Hungary in 1514—77.

D

Dante, Alighieri (1265-1321)—great Italian poet—191.

Diderot, Denis (1713-1784)—outstanding French philosopher, mechanistic materialist, atheist, ideologist of the French revolutionary bourgeoisie, educationalist and distinguished encyclopaedian—196.

Dietrichstein, Siegmund von (1484-1540)—vicegerent in Styria, and commander-in-chief in Styria, Carinthia and Upper Austria; suppressor of peasant insurrection in the Austrian Alps in 1515-1516—77, 123, 124.

Dózsa, Georg (c. 1474-1514)—lesser nobleman of Transylvania's Székler region; leader of peasant uprising in Hungary in 1514; was brutally tortured to death by victorious noblemen—76-77.

Dózsa, Gregor—brother of Georg Dózsa, participant of peasant uprising in Hungary in 1514; taken captive with his brother and executed (1514)—76.

E

Eberstein, Mangold (died in 1517)—offspring of Franconian branch of Ebersteins, a noble family—191.

Eisenhut, Anton—pastor of Eppingen (Palatinate); leader of local peasants and townsmen uprising during Peasant War of 1525; taken captive by Truchsess's punitive expedition and executed in 1525—103.

Eitel, Hans—leader of "Lake Troop" (Swabia) in 1525 Peasant War; signed defeatist Weingarten Agreement with Truchsess, disbanding his troop—88.

Ernst (1464-1513)—Archbishop of Magdeburg (1476-1513)—53.

F

Ferdinand I (1503-1564)—Austrian Archduke, from 1556 German Emperor—85, 111, 113, 123-25.

Feuerbacher, Matern—member of town council and leader of burgher opposition in Gross Bottwar (Württemberg); in 1525 headed "Gay Bright Troop" of insurgent Württemberg peasants and townsmen, utilising his influence to moderate the insurrection; after defeat of insurgents at Böblingen escaped to Switzerland—97, 98, 102.

Florian—see Greisel, Florian.

Forner, Anton—burgomaster of the imperial town of Nördlingen (Franconia); sided with the rebellious peasants in 1525 and headed the plebeian party of his town—92.

Fourier, Francois Charles Marie (1772-1837)—great French Utopian Socialist—22.

Francis I (1494-1547)—King of France (1515-1547)—84.

Frederick II (1712-1786)—King

of Prussia (1740-1786)—160, 161, 193.

Frederick III (1463-1525)— Elector of Saxony (1486-1525) —48.

Frederick William (1620-1688)— Elector of Brandenburg (from 1640)—175.

Frederick William III (1770-1840)—King of Prussia (1797-1840)—160, 175.

Frundsberg, Georg von (1473-1528)—commanded German lansquenets in service of Swabian League; in 1525-1526 took part in suppressing peasant uprising in Swabia and Archbishopric of Salzburg—113, 124.

G

Geismaier, Michael (assassinated in 1527)—son of a miner, one of most active and talented leaders of peasant uprising in Tyrol and Archbishopric of Salzburg; brilliantly directed military operations of insurgent troops in 1525 and 1526 —123, 125.

Georg (1471-1539)—Duke of Saxony (1500-1539), one of organisers of massacre of insurgent peasants in Thuringia in 1525—60.

Gerber, Erasmus—one of main leaders of insurgent peasants in Alsace in 1525; was taken captive and hung after defeat of insurgents at Zabern in 1525—120.

Gerber, Theus—leader of a troop of Stuttgart townsmen who joined Württemberg peasant insurgents under Feuerbacher in 1525; after defeat of uprising escaped to Switzerland— 98, 103.

Geyer, Florian—German knight, went over to insurgent peasants in 1525; headed "Black Troop"; killed in battle in 1525—93-96, 105, 108.

Gluck, Christoph Willibald von (1714-1787)—great German composer—195.

Goethe, Johann Wolfgang von (1749-1832)—great German thinker and writer—167, 195.

Götz—see Berlichingen, Götz.

Grebel, Konrad—leader of Anabaptist sect in Zürich, follower of Münzer; revolutionary agitator in South Germany—62.

Greisel, Florian—priest, active participant of Peasant War of 1525 in Swabia; was in command of Lower Allgäu troop and remnants of Baltringen Troop; routed by Truchsess in early April 1525; after conclusion of Weingarten agreement escaped to Switzerland—101.

Gugel-Bastian—organiser of peasant conspiracy in Margraviate of Baden in 1514; beheaded in Freiburg in 1514—75.

Gustavus I, or *Gustavus Vasa* (1496-1560)—King of Sweden (1523-1560); in 1527 initiated "royal reformation" (making the king Head of the church), confiscating church possessions in favour of treasury and nobility—189

H

Habern, Wilhelm—Marshal of the Palatinate, military leader under Ludwig, the Elector Palatine; took part in suppressing knights' insurrection in 1522-23 and peasant uprising in the Palatinate in 1525—96, 111.

Händel, Georg Friedrich (1685-1759)—great German composer —195.

Hanssen, Georg H. (1809-1894) —German bourgeois economist

and statistician; author of a number of works on history of German agrarian system—174.

Hegel, Georg Wilhelm Friedrich (1770-1831)—distinguished German philosopher, objective idealist; produced the most exhaustive exposition of idealist dialectics—22, 55, 192.

Helfenstein, Count von, Ludwig (c. 1498-1525)—Austrian vicegerent in Weinsberg (Württemberg), notorious for his perfidy and cruelty to peasants; captured by insurgent peasants in 1525 and executed —93, 95, 105.

Henry III (1551-1589)—King of France (1574-1589), last of Valois dynasty. He was killed by a partisan of the Catholic League during one of the religious wars in support of the Huguenots—196.

Henry IV (1553-1610)—King of France (1589-1610), founder of Bourbon dynasty—196.

Herder, Johann Gottfried (1744-1803)—German idealist philosopher, poet, collector of folk songs and literary critic— 195.

Hesse, Landgrave of—see Philip I.

Hipler, Wendel (died in 1526)— German nobleman, in 1525 joined peasant uprising in Franconia; main author of "Heilbronn Programme", in which he anticipated the idea of bourgeois transformation of Germany's social system; escaped after peasant defeat but was arrested in 1526; died in prison—93, 95, 104, 106.

Hohenlohe, Counts von—representatives of a lesser Franconian princely family—93.

Hohenstaufen—dynasty of German emperors (1138-1254)— 189.

Hosszú, Anton—one of leaders of peasant uprising in Hungary in 1514—77.

Hubmaier, Balthasar—pastor of Waldshut in South Germany, doctor of theology, follower of Münzer and preacher of popular Reformation; one of inspirers of insurrection of peasants and townsmen in Black Forest; burnt at the stake in 1528—62, 84.

Hus, John (c. 1369-1415)—outstanding Bohemian reformer, professor of Prague University; his opposition to a number of Catholic dogmas and extortions by Catholic churchmen began broad liberation movement in Bohemia against German clerical and lay feudal lords; accused of heresy by Constance Council and burnt at the stake—44.

Hutten, Frowin von—Ulrich von Hutten's cousin, courtier of Elector of Mayence; in 1525 took part in suppressing peasant insurrection—110.

Hutten, Ulrich von (1488-1523)— German humanitarian and poet; one of ideologists of knighthood and participant of knights' insurrection of 1522-1523—48, 80-82, 110, 168, 169, 171.

I

Ivan III (1440-1505)—Grand Prince of Moscow (from 1462), achieved final liberation of Russia from Mongol-Tatar yoke and in the main completed unification of all Russian lands around Moscow, forming a united national state—188.

J

Joachim the Calabrese, or *Joachim of Floris* (c. 1132-1202)

—Italian mystic, protagonist of "the second coming of Christ" and the "millennium"; the Catholic Church declared his teaching a heresy—53.

Johann (1468-1532)—Duke of Saxony, from 1525 Elector of Saxony; organised reprisals against insurgent peasants in Thuringia in 1525; prominent in the princely reformation—48, 58.

Joss, Fritz (died about 1517)—prominent organiser of secret peasant societies and conspiracies in South Germany in early 16th century—70-72, 76, 170.

K

Kant, Immanuel (1724-1804)—eminent German philosopher, prime exponent of late 18th- and early 19th-century German idealism—195.

Karl-August (1757-1828)—Grand Duke of Saxe-Weimar; took part in campaigns of reactionary German states against revolutionary France—194.

Kautsky, Karl (1854-1938)—German Social-Democrat, publicist, editor of *Neue Zeit* (1883-1917); became Marxist in the 1880s; subsequently an opportunist, championed Centrism in the German Social-Democratic movement and the Second International—176.

Kepler, Johann (1571-1630)—German astronomer—194.

Kindlinger, Nikolaus (1749-1819)—conservative German historian, author of "History of Peasant Dependence in Germany, Particularly of So-Called Serfdom", which appeared in 1818—174.

Knopf of Leubas—see Schmidt, Jörg.

Konrad III (1466-1540)—Bishop of Würzburg (1519-1540); one of organisers of cruel suppression of peasant uprising and movement of urban plebeians in Franconia in 1525—110.

Kovalevsky, Maxim Maximovich (1851-1916)—prominent Russian bourgeois sociologist, historian and jurist; noted for his research on primitive communal system—135.

L

Lamparter, Gregor (1463-1523)—counsellor of Duke Ulrich of Württemberg—74.

Lassalle, Ferdinand (1825-1864)—German Socialist, founder of General Association of German Workers; originated opportunist reformist trend in German working-class movement (Lassalleanism) indefatigably combated by Marx and Engels—167, 169.

Laurentius—see Mészéros, Laurentius.

Leibnitz, Gottfried Wilhelm (1646-1716)—great German mathematician and idealist philosopher—192, 194.

Leonhardt, Adolf (1815-1880)—reactionary Prussian statesman, minister of justice under Bismarck—143.

Lessing, Gotthold Ephraim (1729-1781)—great German writer, critic and philosopher, a prominent 18th-century educationalist—195.

Limburg, Counts of—Franconian nobles—96.

Lorcher—counsellor of Duke Ulrich of Württemberg—74.

Louis XI (1423-1483)—King of France (1461-1483); one of founders of French absolutist monarchy; fought with success for unification of French possessions in a single kingdom.—30, 81, 187.

Löwenstein, Counts von—members of a lesser princely family in Franconia—93.

Ludwig V (1478-1544)—Elector Palatine (1508-1544); took part in suppressing knights' insurrection of 1522-1523; one of chief organisers of reprisals against insurgent peasants in Franconia in 1525; took part in Truchsess's punitive expedition—75, 84, 95, 103, 105, 108.

Luther, Martin (1483-1546)—prominent leader of the Reformation; founded the Protestant (Lutheran) movement in Germany; ideologist of the burghers; sided with the princes against the rebellious peasants and town poor in the Peasant War of 1525—48-54, 58-62, 79, 83.

M

Magdeburg, Archbishop of—see Ernst.

Mantel, Johann (c. 1468-1530)—theologian, preacher in Stuttgart, follower of Münzer—62.

Manteuffel, Otto Theodor (1805-1882)—Prussian statesman, minister of the interior in counter-revolutionary ministry of Brandenburg (1848-1850)—164.

Marx, Karl (1818-1883)—7, 8, 166, 172, 173.

Mätthaus (c. 1468-1540)—Archbishop of Salzburg (from 1519); advocate of persecuting followers of the Reformation, and of reprisals against peasants and townsmen who revolted in 1525 in the Archbishopric of Salzburg—122, 125.

Mauerer, Georg Ludwig von (1790-1872)—German bourgeois historian, student of social system of ancient and medieval Germany—136, 172, 173.

Maximilian I (1459-1519)—Austrian Archduke, German Emperor from 1493—69, 77, 85.

Mehring, Franz (1846-1919)—German Social-Democrat, literary critic and historian, a Left-wing leader of German Social-Democrats; subsequently member of the Spartacus League and the Communist Party of Germany—174.

Meitzen, August (1822-1910)—German bourgeois economist and statistician—163, 165, 174.

Melanchthon, Philip (1497-1560)—German theologian, closest associate of Luther; author of "Augsburg Confession"—59.

Menke, Heinrich Theodor (1819-1892)—German cartographer—181, 193.

Menzingen, Stephan von—German knight; headed insurrection of Rothenburg petty burghers and plebeians against the patriciate; after Rothenburg was occupied by troops of Margrave Casimir of Brandenburg-Ansbach, was executed (1525)—92, 110.

Merovingians—dynasty of Frankish kings (5th-8th centuries)—145.

Mészéros, Laurentius—priest of Szeged; one of leaders of peasant insurrection in Hungary in 1514; captured by Hungarian nobility and executed (1514)—76, 77.

Metzler, Georg—one of leaders of peasant uprising in Odenwald (Franconia), and chief of "Gay Bright Troop"; belonged to moderate party; escaped after defeat of "Gay Bright Troop" at Königshofen—92, 95, 104, 106.

Mozart, Wolfgang Amadeus Gottlieb (1756-1791)—great Austrian composer—195.

Müller, Hans—leader of Black Forest peasants in 1525; chief of Hegau troop; betrayed peasants; executed after defeat of uprising (1525)—84, 85, 88, 112.

Münzer, Thomas (c. 1490-1525)—great German revolutionary, leader and ideologist of the peasant-plebeian camp during the Reformation and the Peasant War of 1525; preached equalitarian utopian communism.—7, 38, 42, 47, 51, 53, 54, 55, 56-62, 69, 79, 84, 86, 88, 104, 114, 116-119, 123, 177.

N

Napoleon I, Bonaparte (1769-1821)—Emperor of the French (1804-1814 and 1815)—150, 161, 196.

Napoleon III (1808-1873)—Emperor of the French (1852-1870)—12.

O

Ottos—German kings and emperors of Saxon dynasty (936-1002)—191.

Otto I (912-973)—German King (from 936), founder and first emperor (from 962) of the Holy Roman Empire—189.

Owen, Robert (1771-1858)—great British Utopian Socialist—22.

P

Palatine, Elector—see Ludwig V.

Pfeifer, Heinrich—one of leaders of uprising of townsmen in Mühlhausen in 1525; executed (1525)—114, 119.

Philip I (1479-1533)—Margrave of Baden; brutally massacred participants of "Union Shoe" conspiracy in 1513; in 1525 took part in suppressing peasant uprising in South Germany—70, 75.

Philip I (1504-1567)—Landgrave of Hesse; took part in suppressing insurrection of knights in 1522-1523; chief suppressor of peasant uprising in Thuringia in 1525—82, 117-19, 126.

Plato (c. 427-347 B. C.)—ancient Greek idealist philosopher, ideologist of the slave-owning aristocracy—176.

Pregizer, Kaspar—cutler in Schorndorf (Württemberg), one of organisers of "Poor Konrad"; took part in uprising of peasants and townsmen in Württemberg in 1514; escaped after uprising was defeated—73.

Prassler, Kaspar—leader of insurgent peasant and miner troops in Salzburg Archbishopric in 1525—123.

R

Rabmann, Franz—preacher in Griessen, South Germany; follower of Münzer and advocate of popular Reformation; took part in uprising of Black Forest and Klettgau peasants and plebeians; cruelly tortured to death after suppression of peasant insurrection (1525)—62.

Richard (1467-1531)—Elector and Archbishop of Trier (1511-1531), bitter opponent of Reformation; took part in suppressing knights' uprising in 1522-1523 and peasant uprising in 1525—82, 111, 168.

Rohrbach, Jäcklein—one of chiefs of peasant uprising in Franconia in 1525; chief of Neckar valley peasants; on Truchsess's order was cruelly executed in 1525—93, 95, 97, 102, 103.

S

Saint-Simon, Claude-Henri, Comte de (1760-1825)—great French Utopian Socialist—22.

Salzburg, Archbishop of—see Mätthaus.

Saxony, Elector of—see Frederik III.

Schappeler, Christoph (1472-1551)—doctor of theology and follower of Münzer; headed plebeian opposition in Memmingen (Upper Swabia) in 1524-1525; escaped after unsuccessful uprising of plebeians in Memmingen—62, 112.

Schiller, Johann Christoph Friedrich (1759-1805)—great German writer—170, 195.

Schlözer, August Ludwig von (1735-1809)—German conservative historian, journalist and statistician—194.

Schmidt, Jörg—known as "Knopf", peasant from Leubas, Upper Swabia; active participant of Peasant War of 1525 and chief of Allgäu troop: fled after defeat of his troop, but was captured, tortured and executed (1526)—114.

Schmidt, Ulrich—ironsmith, leader of Baltringen troop of insurgent Swabian peasants in 1525—88.

Schneider, Georg—former captain of lansquenets in French service; took part in "Union Shoe" conspiracy and preparations of abortive peasant insurrection in Rhineland in 1513—71.

Schön, Ulrich—participant of Peasant War of 1525, chief of Leipheim troop of Swabian insurgent peasants; after defeat of his troop was captured and executed at Truchsess's order (1525)—89, 100.

Schubart, Johann Christian (1734-1787)—German agronomist—194.

Shakespeare, William (1564-1616)—great English writer—170.

Sickingen, Franz von (1481-1523)—German knight, joined Reformation; leader of knights' insurrection in 1522-1523—48, 80, 84, 128, 167-71.

Singerhans—Württemberg peasant; one of leaders of "Poor Konrad" and peasant uprising in Württemberg and mountain regions of Swabia in 1514—73.

Spät, Dietrich (died in 1536)—German nobleman, leader of a detachment of Truchsess's punitive expedition; took part in suppressing peasant uprising in 1925—99, 102, 106.

Spruner, Karl (1803-1892)—German historian and cartographer—181.

Stoffel (from Freiburg)—one of organisers of "Union Shoe" peasant conspiracy in Upper Rhineland and Black Forest in 1513; escaped after conspiracy was discovered — 71.

Storch, Niklas—weaver from Zwickau, headed Anabaptist sect; under Münzer's influence preached popular insurrection against clerical and lay feudal lords—53.

Sulz, Rudolph, Count von—judge of imperial court in Rottweil; owner of Klettgau; one of organisers of reprisals against insurgent peasants in South Germany during Peasant War of 1525—112.

Száleresi, Ambros—Pest townsman, joined peasant uprising in Hungary in 1514; appointed

NAME INDEX

chief of one of peasant troops, but with a group of townsmen betrayed the peasant insurgents and went over to nobility—76.

T

Tacitus, Publius Cornelius (c. 55-c. 120)—prominent Roman historian—139.

Teleki, István—counsellor of the king, later Hungarian treasurer; killed by insurgents during peasant uprising of 1514—77.

Thumb, Konrad (1465-1525)—counsellor of Duke Ulrich of Württemberg—74.

Thunfeld, Kunz von—German knight, vassal of Bishop of Würzburg; participant of peasant conspiracy of Hans Böheim in Niklashausen (Bishopric of Würzburg) in 1476—65.

Thunfeld, Michael—son of Kunz von Thunfeld; together with his father took part in peasant conspiracy of Hans Böheim in Niklashausen in 1476—65.

Treves, Archbishop of—see Richard.

Truchsess, Georg (1488-1531)—commanded armed forces of Swabian League, chief suppressor and executioner of peasant uprising in 1525—85, 88, 89, 93, 100-10, 113, 118.

Tudor—dynasty of English kings (1485-1603)—188.

Tyler, Wat—leader of peasant uprising in England in 1381; roofer, treacherously killed in 1381 by feudal lords during negotiations between insurgent peasants and King Richard II—44.

U

Ulrich (1487-1550)—Duke of Württemberg (from 1498); suppressed peasant uprising in Württemberg in 1514 (insurrection of "Poor Konrad"); in 1519 was banished by nobility and burghers discontent with his policy; attempted to utilise peasant movement of 1525 to restore his power; in 1534 regained Württemberg—73-75, 87, 88, 89.

V

Vasco da Gama (1469-1524)—Portuguese navigator, discovered the sea route to India round the Cape of Good Hope (1497-1498)—28.

Voltaire, Francois Marie Arouet de (1694-1778)—French philosopher, deist, satirical writer, historian, eminent bourgeois 18th-century educationalist, opposed absolutism and Catholicism—196.

W

Wehe, Jakob—pastor from Leipheim, follower of Münzer: in 1525 one of leaders of Leipheim peasant troop, after whose defeat he was executed (1525)—62, 89, 93, 100.

Weigand, Bishop of Bamberg (1522-1556)—one of organisers of massacre of insurgent peasants in Franconia in 1525—110.

Weitmoser, Erasmus—prosperous artisan from Hastein (Archduchy of Salzburg) and leader of a troop of Salzburg miners and peasants during uprising of 1525—123.

Wellington, Sir Arthur Wellesley, Duke of (1769-1852)—186.

Welsers—a family of Augsburg merchants and bankers; in 15th and 16th centuries owned metallurgical and other industries in South Germany; large-scale traders and usurers, creditors of many European monarchs—85.

Wieland, Christoph Martin (1733-1813)—German bourgeois 18th-century educationalist and writer—195.

Wilhelm (c. 1470-1541)—Bishop of Strassburg (1506-1541); in 1525 took part in quelling peasant insurrection in Bishopric of Mayence—110.

William I (1797-1888)—Prussian King (1861-1888) and German Emperor (1871-1888)—175.

Wolff, Wilhelm (1809-1864)—outstanding German proletarian revolutionary, member of Central Committee of Communist League, member of editorial board of *Neue Rheinische Zeitung;* pupil, comrade-in-arms and close friend of Marx and Engels—162.

Würzburg, Bishop of—see Conrad III.

Wycliffe, John (c. 1320-1384)—English religious reformer; fought for creation of an English church independent from Rome, and a reform of Catholicism; opposed sale of indulgences; the Catholic Church denounced him as a heretic—44, 45.

Z

Zimmermann, Wilhelm (1807-1878)—German historian, petty-bourgeois democrat; son of an artisan; pastor and history teacher in Stuttgart; took part in 1848 revolution, deputy of Frankfurt Parliament, in which he belonged to extreme Left faction; author of "History of the Peasants' War in Germany", and other works—7, 58.

Zápolya, Johann (1487-1540)—Transylvanian Voivode; suppressed peasant uprising in Hungary in 1514; in 1526 was made King of Hungary—76.